DAD—

Thanks for your support through this entire project.

Love—

John

Baseball
One Helluva Life

DAVE ROSENFIELD

as told to

JOHN TRAUB

∾INFINITY
PUBLISHING

Copyright © 2012 by John Traub

ISBN 978-0-7414-7616-6 Paperback
ISBN 978-0-7414-7810-8 Hardcover
ISBN 978-0-7414-7617-3 eBook

Printed in the United States of America

Published August 2012

INFINITY PUBLISHING
1094 New DeHaven Street, Suite 100
West Conshohocken, PA 19428-2713
Toll-free (877) BUY BOOK
Local Phone (610) 941-9999
Fax (610) 941-9959
Info@buybooksontheweb.com
www.buybooksontheweb.com

CONTENTS

Dedications iii

Preface vii

Chapter One: *Who I Am* 1

Chapter Two: *My Formative Years* 9

Chapter Three: *The Early Years* 21

Chapter Four: *Giving It A Shot* 39

Chapter Five: *In The Navy* 45

Chapter Six: *My Star-Crossed Life* 63

Chapter Seven: *Beginning In Bakersfield* 79

Chapter Eight: *Somewhere Over The Rainbow* 99

Chapter Nine: *Virginia Is For Baseball Lovers* 105

Chapter Ten: *Meet The Mets* 135

Chapter Eleven: *On The Radio* 157

Chapter Twelve: *Friends And Colleagues* 169

Chapter Fourteen: *An Awakening* 205

Chapter Fifteen: *Charmaine* 211

Chapter Sixteen: *A Whole New Ball Game* 219

Chapter Seventeen: *The New York Mess* 227

Chapter Eighteen: *Introspection* 233

Epilogue 239

Index 255

DEDICATIONS

From Dave Rosenfield

I have no idea how someone can choose a single person for a dedication. I guess if you write multiple books you can spread it around, or if you have a short and simple life, there may not be a problem. My long and eventful life causes me to dedicate this book to so many people that have helped me along the way and made my life full of fun and excitement that I cannot mention them each by name.

To my folks for the true understanding that they gave to each of their children, the life lessons that we thought at the time sounded preachy, and the good genes they provided to keep me on the right side of the grass for these many decades.

To Mata, who was my friend and an ever-patient wife for the formative years of my career and left this earth too soon, and Marc, who fulfilled what every man wants, a son that is a good and honorable man, who has become a great father and husband and has made me proud every day.

To Charmaine, who I knew first as a business friend, and then when she later came into my personal life, filled a void, and helped me to be a much better person for having known and loved her. She also provided a new and extended family that has enriched our lives.

To the people I have worked for, from Joe Gannon in Bakersfield who gave me my start, to Dick Davis, an amazing man that became a boss, a mentor and more than a dear friend, and to Ken Young who disproved the old axiom that "you can't teach an old dog new tricks."

To the managers and coaches of my younger days who taught me how baseball should be played, and cemented my love and respect for the game, and the managers and coaches that I have had the privilege of working with in professional baseball that are among the best friends of my life.

To all the people whom I have worked with in these 50-plus seasons, who have provided the network that has enabled me to live "a life without a job", but instead a life of fun and entertainment every day.

And lastly, to John Traub who had the patience to listen and chronicle the endless stories of a guy who loves to tell them.

From John Traub

To my family – Liz (for your eyes and ears), Joe and Sophie (for letting me use the computer), and Walter (for getting up with me at 5:00 am)

To Kris Shepard – for the input and cartoon drawings

To Ian Locke - for helping acquire so many great photos

To Ken Young – for keeping Dave and hiring me

To Dave Rosenfield - for trusting me to help tell the stories of his life

TIMELINE OF MY LIFE

1929	Born in El Paso, TX
1936	Family moved to Los Angeles, CA
1938	Listened to first baseball game on radio
1939	Attended first professional baseball game
1945	Almost died after being hit by a car
1947	Graduated LA High; accepted baseball scholarship to UCLA
1950	Signed contract with Philadelphia Phillies
1951	Dad died in January; Entered Navy in November
1956	Graduated LA State in January; Hired as general manager of Bakersfield Boosters in February; married Mata in April
1957	Marc was born
1958	Named California League Executive of the Year
1961	Hired as general manager of Topeka Reds
1962	Hired as asst. general manager of Tidewater Tides
1963	Organized Tidewater Community Baseball; named GM of Tides
1968	Also ran Norfolk Neptunes of Continental Football League
1969	Tides moved up to Triple-A; affiliate with New York Mets
1970	Tides moved into Met Park
1974	Served as interim GM of ABA's Virginia Squires
1975	Mom died; named International League Executive of the Year; GM of Tidewater Sharks of Southern Hockey League
1977	Named vice president of International League
1982	Named International League Executive of the Year
1987	Named International League Executive of the Year
1991	Mata died
1992	Married Charmaine
1993	Tides moved into Harbor Park; team purchased by Ken Young's group; Tides won John H. Johnson Award; Named International League Executive of the Year
1994	Tides won Bob Freitas Award
1998	Inducted into Tidewater Shrine
2004	Named Minor League Baseball's "King of Baseball"
2006	Celebrated 50th year in Minor League Baseball
2007	Tides ended 38-year affiliation with Mets; started affiliation with Orioles
2008	Inducted in International League Hall of Fame
2009	Inducted into Hampton Roads Sports Hall of Fame
2011	Celebrated 50th year with Tides; had heart valve replaced; received Presidential Citation from Minor League Baseball
2012	Stepped back from day-to-day operation of Tides and named Vice President/Senior Advisor; honored by Norfolk Sports Club with Lifetime Achievement Award

MY BASEBALL CARD

Year	Club	League (Class.)	MLB Club	Field Manager
1956	Bakersfield Boosters	California (C)	Phillies	Art Lilly/Dick Wilson
1957	Bakersfield Bears	California (C)	Cubs	Dick Wilson/Babe Herman
1958	Bakersfield Bears	California (C)	Phillies	Paul Owens
1959	Bakersfield Bears	California (C)	Phillies	Paul Owens
1960	Bakersfield Bears	California (C)	Phillies	Lou Kahn
1961	Topeka Reds	Three-I (B)	Reds	Dave Bristol
1962	Tidewater Tides	So. Atlantic (AA)	Cardinals	Chase Riddle
1963	Tidewater Tides	Carolina (A)	Independent	Al Jones
1964	Tidewater Tides	Carolina (A)	White Sox	Al Jones
1965	Tidewater Tides	Carolina (A)	White Sox	Al Jones
1966	Tidewater Tides	Carolina (A)	Phillies	Bobby Morgan/Lou Kahn
1967	Tidewater Tides	Carolina (A)	Phillies	Bob Wellman
1968	Tidewater Tides	Carolina (A)	Phillies	Bob Wellman
1969	Tidewater Tides	Int'l (AAA)	Mets	Clyde McCullough
1970	Tidewater Tides	Int'l (AAA)	Mets	Chuck Hiller
1971	Tidewater Tides	Int'l (AAA)	Mets	Hank Bauer
1972	Tidewater Tides	Int'l (AAA)	Mets	Hank Bauer
1973	Tidewater Tides	Int'l (AAA)	Mets	John Antonelli
1974	Tidewater Tides	Int'l (AAA)	Mets	John Antonelli
1975	Tidewater Tides	Int'l (AAA)	Mets	Joe Frazier
1976	Tidewater Tides	Int'l (AAA)	Mets	Tom Burgess
1977	Tidewater Tides	Int'l (AAA)	Mets	Frank Verdi
1978	Tidewater Tides	Int'l (AAA)	Mets	Frank Verdi
1979	Tidewater Tides	Int'l (AAA)	Mets	Frank Verdi
1980	Tidewater Tides	Int'l (AAA)	Mets	Frank Verdi
1981	Tidewater Tides	Int'l (AAA)	Mets	Jack Aker
1982	Tidewater Tides	Int'l (AAA)	Mets	Jack Aker
1983	Tidewater Tides	Int'l (AAA)	Mets	Davey Johnson
1984	Tidewater Tides	Int'l (AAA)	Mets	Bob Schaefer
1985	Tidewater Tides	Int'l (AAA)	Mets	Bob Schaefer
1986	Tidewater Tides	Int'l (AAA)	Mets	Sam Perlozzo
1987	Tidewater Tides	Int'l (AAA)	Mets	Mike Cubbage
1988	Tidewater Tides	Int'l (AAA)	Mets	Mike Cubbage
1989	Tidewater Tides	Int'l (AAA)	Mets	Mike Cubbage
1990	Tidewater Tides	Int'l (AAA)	Mets	Steve Swisher
1991	Tidewater Tides	Int'l (AAA)	Mets	Steve Swisher
1992	Tidewater Tides	Int'l (AAA)	Mets	Clint Hurdle
1993	Norfolk Tides	Int'l (AAA)	Mets	Clint Hurdle
1994	Norfolk Tides	Int'l (AAA)	Mets	Bobby Valentine
1995	Norfolk Tides	Int'l (AAA)	Mets	Toby Harrah
1996	Norfolk Tides	Int'l (AAA)	Mets	Bobby Valentine/Bruce Benedict
1997	Norfolk Tides	Int'l (AAA)	Mets	Rick Dempsey
1998	Norfolk Tides	Int'l (AAA)	Mets	Rick Dempsey
1999	Norfolk Tides	Int'l (AAA)	Mets	John Gibbons
2000	Norfolk Tides	Int'l (AAA)	Mets	John Gibbons
2001	Norfolk Tides	Int'l (AAA)	Mets	John Gibbons
2002	Norfolk Tides	Int'l (AAA)	Mets	Bobby Floyd
2003	Norfolk Tides	Int'l (AAA)	Mets	Bobby Floyd
2004	Norfolk Tides	Int'l (AAA)	Mets	John Stearns
2005	Norfolk Tides	Int'l (AAA)	Mets	Ken Oberkfell
2006	Norfolk Tides	Int'l (AAA)	Mets	Ken Oberkfell
2007	Norfolk Tides	Int'l (AAA)	Orioles	Gary Allenson
2008	Norfolk Tides	Int'l (AAA)	Orioles	Gary Allenson
2009	Norfolk Tides	Int'l (AAA)	Orioles	Gary Allenson
2010	Norfolk Tides	Int'l (AAA)	Orioles	Gary Allenson/Bobby Dickerson
2011	Norfolk Tides	Int'l (AAA)	Orioles	Gary Allenson
2012	Norfolk Tides	Int'l (AAA)	Orioles	Ron Johnson

PREFACE

Written by John Traub

If you are reading this book, you probably know Dave Rosenfield. You may not know that you know him, but it's likely that you do. You may know *of* him, but chances are, you don't *really* know the man who has carved out an iconic career and reputation in the true grass-roots level of the great American pastime – minor league baseball.

Dave Rosenfield, by his own description, has "had an interesting life." It's quite the understatement from a man whose grandfather was a Confederate captain during the Civil War, whose mother was an actress who worked with Groucho Marx and Charlie Chaplin, whose father was involved in the starting of the Piggly Wiggly grocery store chain and whose sister was the editor of one of the first newspapers in the United States to print color photographs. It's quite the understatement from a man whose passion for his profession has kept him working in baseball since the Dodgers were in Brooklyn.

This is a book of Dave's stories, or at least *a lot* of his stories. It's not really possible to tell *every* story of his life or of his career. If you know Dave, you know it's possible for him to tell the stories. The difficult task in writing this book was trying to determine which of these stories made the final cut. Some stories have to make the book because they're too hilarious to leave out, some stories can't make the book because we aren't sure if kids will be reading this book and some stories won't make it because the binding on the book can only be so-wide.

All of these stories are intertwined and combined to unveil the story of Dave Rosenfield's life. One story leads to another, digresses on another and causes Dave to remember the highlights and lowlights, of his so-called "interesting" life. We should all be so "interesting." The people he's known, the places he's been, the things that he's done, the situations he's found himself in – they're priceless. They tell the story of an octogenarian whose family provided his roots and whose colleagues provided the branches that his life has touched. "Rosie," as he is affectionately known, is an oak tree that has lots of stories carved into its bark. And speaking of bark, well that's one of Dave's attributes we'll get into later.

In the coming pages, Dave tells you – in the first person – the story of his life. You will meander through the chronology of his personal and professional story. You will go with Dave as he digresses into his journey. He digresses quite often, but he doesn't live in the past. In life and in print, he often ties one story to another with a simple phrase: "*But I digress.*" I hope you become enthralled with a living legend that is truly larger than life.

Dave Rosenfield soon after the opening of old Met Park in 1970

CHAPTER ONE

WHO I AM

I killed a woman …

I drove a guy to prison …

I played baseball against Jackie Robinson …

I nearly played the role of Lou Gehrig in "The Pride of the Yankees."

And I don't think that these are *the most* interesting stories in my life.

Throughout my eighty-plus years on this earth, and nearly six decades working in minor league baseball, I've had some unbelievable experiences. I've had an amazing life and I feel very fortunate to have been able to live long enough to share some of my stories with you. I've often been asked to talk about the people whom I've known along the way, about the things I've been involved in and about my life working in minor league baseball. People have told me for years that I should write a book about my life in baseball.

I finally decided that that was a good idea and, during the process, I realized there are probably many things that people don't know about me. You may think of me in a certain way. You may like me, or you may not. That's okay with me and this book probably won't change your opinion of me. But I have tried to live my life with integrity and by doing what I think is the right thing. Whether people agree with me or if they don't, you'll have to search long and far to find anyone who can honestly say that I screwed them over.

And I think that's a pretty good epitaph for anyone to have.

I'm not as big of a horse's ass as some people may think I am.

People may think I'm an ass because I believe certain things are important and I don't vary from that. I'm a great believer in honesty and integrity and I guess when it comes to some of those things, I'm stubborn. I remember my dad Leon saying, "You can lose your money. You can lose your health. You can lose everything you own. But you can only lose your integrity if you want to lose it." I prize that saying and have never forgotten it.

People may think I'm an ass because I don't give up and give in on those things. I will compromise on a lot of things, but I'll never compromise on honesty or integrity. I believe people think I'm hard, unyielding, and I don't think that I am. I think that, if things are reasonable, I can be convinced to do it another way. I think the employees who have been with me any length of time have a great deal of respect for me and they know that I'm fair. I may not do everything they want, but they know I'm fair. And to me, that's the most important thing you can be with anybody.

I know I have a reputation of being a person who really wants things to be done right. Being a perfectionist isn't the right word. Nothing needs to be perfect, but it ought to approach it. I try to stay completely abreast of everything that's going on. I hate surprises. If we've got a problem, I want to know about it. That way, if somebody says something to me about it, I already know. I probably have a reputation of being very tough to work for, and I don't believe it's true. Because I don't think I could have people stay with me as long as they have if I really was that way. There are people I've had with me for almost forty years.

I don't think my expectations in people are unreasonable. I probably expect more of myself than I do of anybody else, but I expect people to try. I am as displeased with myself if I make a mistake as I am with anyone else, or perhaps more so. As I tell people, make all the mistakes you want. Once. If you're going to make a mistake, make a new one. If you keep making the same old ones, it tells me either you're not very smart, or you're not trying. The thing is, if I'm upset and air something out, it's over with. I don't hold grudges and I think I'm fair. I try very hard to be fair.

In this day and time, people who take great pride in their jobs are jewels. When I started working in professional baseball, I think people took more pride in their work. I have tried to explain to young people about the difference between a job and a career. Until you stop and think about it, a lot of people don't understand there's a major difference. I say that if this is a job, it's a horseshit job. You work a lot of hours, particularly when you start. You work a tremendous number of hours and don't get paid a lot. And often people don't appreciate you very much. But if it's a career, it's a great career. It's a huge difference.

The last thing I want to hear from a young person I'm interviewing is how much they love baseball. I tell them that loving baseball isn't going to do them any good because they aren't going to see a lot of baseball. I see baseball. They don't. I've been in baseball for 57 years. It took me a lot of years before I got to see a lot of baseball, because when the game's going on, that's when you're working.

I am not a guy who watches the clock. Even now, after all these years, I often will work 12-hour days or even longer. If I have employees who watch the clock, I don't have them for very long. I had a young guy years ago whose office was within view from my office. Every time I looked in his office, I'd see him staring up at the clock. It would bother the shit out of me. I finally went into his office one day, took the clock down and stomped on it. He lasted one season with me and I had to let him go.

Even when I was in college, I had a job at a printer's ink company where I was supposed to punch a time clock when I got to work, when I went to lunch, when I got back, when I went home. I would miss anywhere from two to four of the punch-ins or punch-outs daily. The time clock has just always bothered me. My boss would tell me I had to use the clock because the auditors would question how much they were paying me. But the whole regimentation of it really got to me. And the concept of people being so concerned with having worked a certain set number of hours per day is really a problem for me.

I have a reputation for hating kids, which I don't. I hate kids that misbehave by throwing stuff, or who annoy the other fans. We used to use condiments in the individual packets, and kids would take great delight in putting them on the ground and stomping on them and shooting ketchup and mustard and relish on walls and everywhere else. That used to drive me crazy.

I've always kind of viewed my baseball stadium as my home. And I think there's a certain level of expectation for how people should behave, especially kids. Would you let people behave that way in your house? There are not that many people that say, "Yes I would." I think that when people have paid an admission price, they are entitled to think of it as their house. Paying customers have that right. Not to be unreasonable, but we try very hard to let people know it's not acceptable when things are offensive to people around them. I think by and large, paying customers appreciate that. I think there should be a kind of decorum at a stadium. I know that's a pretty highfalutin word for a baseball stadium, but it's what I believe. If kids sneak in and just watch the game without causing problems, that doesn't bother me because that's how I started loving baseball.

Some kids may tend to disagree with my explanation of why I don't like them. One day at Frank D. Lawrence Stadium in the mid-1960s, I saw a kid who was probably about 10 years old attempting to squeeze his way through the iron bars in one of the closed gates. The bars were spaced such that if a child could get his head through the bars, the rest of their body would easily follow. I saw this kid and he got everything through but his head. His rear end was towards me. I said something and he gave me some smart remark and -- I should have resisted but I didn't. I kicked him right in the butt and almost sent him back through the bars. One of our off-duty policemen was standing right there and he said, "I'm not going to say anything, but I don't think that was a very good idea."

I think my size has a lot to do with the way people perceive me. I think people who know me know that my size is part of my persona. And my booming voice contributes to my reputation as well. Plus I can be pretty opinionated. I'm seldom at a loss for words. I've always had a pretty good ability to express myself. I think being articulate with a strong voice is a pretty good combination. People tend to listen. I know I scare kids. Even my own grandchildren were scared of me when they were small. People probably have a difficult time saying no to me because they might be intimidated.

But I haven't always been big. When I started in this business in 1956, I weighed around 180 pounds. I used to exercise a lot – playing golf, catching batting practice. I played baseball, handball and basketball most of my life. I was very active. But I never liked exercise for the sake of exercise. I always liked doing something that had some competition. Working out in a gym was something I never wanted to do. I guess over the years with everything I was working on and needing to spend time with my family, I just didn't have a lot of time for exercising.

Gradually, I ate my way to this size. I got very big for a while and probably peaked at about 380 pounds. In this business, you spend a lot of time eating on the run. My two favorite foods in the world are bacon and hot dogs. I used to always keep hot dogs in the fridge at home and eat them as snacks right out of the package. A lot of time I just put them on a plate with a little bit of salt and a little bit of mustard. Sometimes I'd add cocktail sauce. I'd have a quick snack and eat two or four hot dogs. I'd eat a pound of bacon without thinking about it. I'd love putting raw hamburger on saltine crackers as a snack.

We are in so many social situations all the time in this industry that it's easy to have a couple of drinks every day. I was able to handle drinking at a pretty good capacity but I guess I was fortunate that it never got away from me. It's not like I was ever falling down making an idiot of myself.

I was also a heavy smoker for a long time. I'd smoke as many as four packs a day for many years.

Boy … I guess I am lucky to be alive.

While I am baring my soul, it's a relief to finally admit that I am not the age everyone has always thought I've been. During the 2011 season, the Norfolk Tides front office threw a huge surprise party for me to celebrate my 50th year with the Tides and my 80th birthday. I guess the surprise was really on them, because it was really my 82nd birthday.

Me with the Triple-A Championship trophy in 1983

CHAPTER TWO

MY FORMATIVE YEARS

I hate liver.

Growing up as the youngest child in a family of eight kids, I was taught at an early age to speak my mind, to stand up for what I believe. And as one of only two boys in the house, I knew that if I wanted to be heard, I had to speak with compassion and conviction. It was about fairness and we all had the same kind of rights. My parents always told us that we had a right to say what we wanted. Despite me being a little kid who didn't know much of what I was saying, they maintained that I had as much right to speak at the dinner table as anybody else.

We never had food served family-style. The food was always plated in the kitchen and was brought into the dining room. You had to eat everything on your plate. If you wanted more, you got more of everything. My parents were very strict. If you didn't finish it, it would be there for you at the next meal. I can remember a couple of my sisters who were as stubborn as hell would be staring at the same food for two, three days. I never realized that there were small cans of anything. We always had those huge number ten cans they use in restaurants.

One night, I was probably five or so, we were served liver for dinner. I hated liver and I noticed that my dad wasn't eating liver. He was having something else. I said to my mother, "You always tell me that we have to do the same thing as everyone else. I hate liver and I see Pop not eating it."

My mother said, "Yeah?"

"Well," I remember saying, "if he doesn't have to eat liver, why do I?"

In typical Estelle Therese Rosenfield fashion, she told me, "You don't have to eat liver again."

I thought that was pretty neat.

My family was probably a little ahead of its time, especially prior to and during the Depression. We had a certain degree of wealth, at least for a while, because of my father's job. My father Leon Rosenfield owned several grocery stores in El Paso, Texas and Las Cruces, New Mexico. He was a well-known member of the business and political communities. He was an alderman in El Paso and was very involved in the community. He was very loyal to his customers. Even at the height of the Depression he wouldn't let anyone go hungry. He allowed people to run tabs in his stores. It was just the kind of man he was.

Back in 1916, Clarence Saunders, a friend of Pop who wanted to start a chain of full-service grocery stores, approached my father. Clarence didn't have the funding or the ability to get the required financing. So he came to my dad knowing that Pop would be able to help him get the financing to start the business. Clarence was wise to come to my dad, but Clarence also had other intentions. The original plan called for them to split their stores into two regions. Clarence was going to have east Texas and Leon was going to get west Texas. But as it turned out, my dad got west Texas and Clarence got the rest of the world.

Thus, the Piggly Wiggly grocery store chain was established. For the next 20 years, Pop owned seven stores in El Paso and one in Las Cruces. There were only four other Safeway and A&P stores combined in these communities, so my dad was the main guy there for a long time.

Pop made a good living. We always had money, but being so young, I never really thought we were defined by wealth. We always had people around - servants, cooks, maids, gardeners, and drivers. I never thought anything of it. My dad felt a strong sense of responsibility to provide for his large family. With eight kids spanning 18 years apart, everyone was at different stages in their lives. I'm sure some of my older siblings grew to have certain levels of expectations because of money. We had a summer home in Cloudcroft, New Mexico, which was like a summer camp just for our family. We had eight kids, two parents and all these helpers.

A family photo from 1931. From left to right – Pop, Julie, Louise, Mary, Dellie (sitting on floor), Nancy, Jo, Mom, Leon and me

I was the baby. I was born on June 13, 1929, right at the start of the Depression. My only brother, Leon Jr., was born eighteen years earlier than me in 1911. It was very unusual in the Jewish religion for a son to share the same name as his father. But I guess we were an unusual family. I had six sisters, each who probably thought of me as a play thing who they could boss around and push around as they pleased.

My parents really believed in letting each of us be whomever we wanted to be, and nobody would judge anyone else because of their beliefs, whether political or in any other area. Just before World War II, when there was a great deal of sympathy for Russia when it was attacked by Hitler, and when the Labor movement in the U.S. was in the public eye as the country worked to come out of the Depression, three of my sisters became members of the Communist Party, and none of the family batted an eye. On the other hand, some members of my family were rather conservative and the wide divergence in political beliefs never caused any friction between us.

Another one of my sisters, Jo, was the first female editor of the UCLA student newspaper and went on to become managing editor of the *Daytona Beach News Journal*. I have two sisters, Nancy and Mary, who are still living well into their nineties. I'm still the baby brother.

I grew up in a very interesting family. My great grandfather Moses Rosenfelder was born in Germany in 1797 and lived until he was 72. Legend has it that my grandfather Julius, who was a Confederate captain during the Civil War, ran a blockade of Mobile Bay in a sailboat to get married. Julius had nine children, several of whom perished in the Galveston flood of 1900 that killed like 10,000 people. The only aunt I ever knew lived well into her nineties and lived near Carnegie Hall in New York City.

Mom and Pop

My parents had great standards. We were taught to do the right thing. We learned about the importance of honesty, commitment and confidence.

We were sort of religious when I was a child. Mom and Pop were both Jewish and they sent all of us to Sunday school to get a Hebrew education. I didn't like a lot of things about Sunday school. The way it was being taught didn't make a lot of sense to me. It was hard for me, and still is I guess, to just accept things based on faith. I need to have things proven to me. I told my parents I didn't want to go to Sunday school any more, and they let me stop going. That was kind of surprising to me. Pop would preside over some of the Jewish ceremonies at home. The prayer book would have Hebrew in phonetic form. It was very hard for us to listen to because my dad really struggled with it. Pop doing phonetic Hebrew with *a deep southern drawl?* We had a hell of a time not laughing. My mother could not resist. We all laughed all the time and would catch a lot of hell because of it.

I was probably four or five years old here

But I digress.

The Piggly Wiggly stores were doing well and my dad was too. Unfortunately, not everyone was cut from the same cloth. The manager my dad had put in charge of running the business embezzled $500,000 from his stores, which in 1935 was all the money in the world. Dad was devastated. He was forced to sell the company and, as part of the transaction, he signed a non-compete clause that prohibited him from opening another store within fifty or a hundred miles. All of his old customers would have come to him, but he wasn't allowed to have a store in those communities. So in 1936 and at the age of fifty six, Pop started over and we moved to California. I was only seven years old and didn't really know the effect this whole thing had on him. My sister Mary, who was 18 then and who is ninety three now and still living in Taos, New Mexico, says that dad went through a terrible depression and looked at it as a personal failure. She says he felt a tremendous amount of guilt because here he had produced eight children and now he wouldn't be able to take care of them as he assumed he would. To suddenly have the world pulled out from under him was so horrible for him.

My dad was a hero to me. I'm not sure I ever wanted to be just like him, but I thought he was a pretty perfect man. He was a living, breathing example of someone who lost everything but his honesty and integrity. He lost all of his money, lost his position, lost everything. But he never became a bad guy. When we got to California, he started out as a food rep and really struggled with that.

He knew the grocery business about as well as anyone could, but at the height of the Depression, he wasn't able to get any kind of decent job. He worked as a food rep for a while and then some people he knew opened a supermarket and they hired him to handle all of their business affairs. After a few years there, he switched jobs and went to work for Sam Given, a man he knew from El Paso. Mr. Given owned Given Machinery Company in Los Angeles and he hired dad to handle the office and the accounting and to handle all the hiring of the employees. The company became known as the first manufacturer of "The Waste King" – the first successful garbage disposal.

After living most of his life with just one kidney, Dad passed away of uremic poisoning in January 1951 at the age of seventy. When my father died, my brother was so broken up; he couldn't handle much of anything. My brother was a very efficient guy. He had worked with my dad in the grocery business and I guess he kind of came apart. And somehow I didn't. So I ended up having to handle all the funeral arrangements and everything at the age of twenty. It was really tough for me. I was the only kid living at home when my dad died.

I was really proud of my mother also. When I was six months old, she suffered a severe skull fracture in an automobile accident and she was bedridden for two years while she recovered. By the time that she recovered, we didn't have any more help around the house and we were going to move to California. She had always wanted to become an actress, so after we moved, she went to the Pasadena Playhouse. It was a breeding ground for young actors and actresses. She'd take the Pacific Electric streetcars by herself at night from Los Angeles to Pasadena and would come home at midnight after rehearsing and performing.

When I was about ten years old, I went to a show my mother was in one night. When the show was over I went back stage to see her. It was dark and as I opened the door, there stood John Carradine, who looked like he was 11 feet tall. He had this mane of hair and there was a little bit of light behind him. Here stood this wraith. He scared the *bejesus* out of me! I screamed and scared the crap out of him.

But I digress.

Mom became a character actress under the stage name Therese Lyon and had some small speaking parts in approximately 40 movies and television shows. She acted with some of Hollywood's greatest names. Her resume included credited and non-credited roles in the "Twilight Zone," "Alfred Hitchcock Presents," "The Loretta Young Show," "The Cisco Kid," "All My Sons," and "The Killers." She played in Groucho Marx's "Time for Elizabeth" on Broadway at the age of sixty four. She also had a recurring role in a national radio program called "The Mayor of the Town" starring Lionel Barrymore and Agnes Moorehead.

She worked with Charlie Chaplin when he was directing and acting in "Monsieur Verdoux" in 1947. She played a housekeeper in a French farm house. While they were getting ready to shoot a scene, my mom said, "Mr.

Chaplin, no French farm house would be complete without a large pot of soup on the stove!"

Chaplin replied, "'Ms. Lyon, you are right." He stopped everything. He stopped production with eight million people working. "Got to find a pot. Got to find some soup!"

He liked my mother so much that he kept her on the payroll for like another week.

She was in this movie in 1946 called "The Strangler of the Swamp." She had this terrible line in the movie. "I want a roof over my head when I pray." It was a terrible movie. My friends mocked me. Whatever a 'B' movie was, this was about a 'G' movie.

The last movie she ever made was "The Music Man" in 1962 at the age of seventy five.

Mom was an artist, having attended art school in St. Louis as a young girl. She loved painting and drawing and ultimately was the host of a one-woman art show. In her final years in the 1970s, she became legally blind but that didn't stop her. One of her last Christmases, she made approximately 200 hand-painted Christmas cards. She used high intensity light and a magnifying glass. She really was a remarkable woman.

After my dad died, mom never looked at another man. She was very, very dominant. My dad was a tough ol' guy, but if she had died first, he wouldn't have lasted six months. He was totally dependent upon her emotionally.

When my mother got sick at the age of eighty eight in 1975 and everyone was at the hospital, I was the last one to get there. I went in to see her and she was kind of comatose. I held her hand and talked to her a little bit, and shortly thereafter, she passed away with me at her side. My family and the doctors said it was like she was waiting for me to get there. She was hanging on to say goodbye to me.

My mother surrounded by many of her paintings and drawings

My parents

CHAPTER THREE

THE EARLY YEARS

I was nine years old in 1938 and had never heard baseball on the radio. I had never attended a game in person. Nationally televised games were still years away from becoming a reality. So I had never really been introduced to baseball. My dad was listening to the World Series between the Yankees and Cubs. I was sitting on the floor with no earthly idea what he was listening to. I sat there listening with him and would ask him a lot of questions. He answered all of my questions and I found it pretty fascinating. That's when I started getting interested in baseball.

When the next spring came around, the Major Leagues were still nearly twenty years from heading to the west coast. At the time, the Pacific Coast League was our big leagues. The Los Angeles Angels and the Hollywood Stars were the closest things to the major leagues we would see, outside of spring training that was held throughout southern California.

My brother Leon was assistant director at a home for kids. He was taking a group of them to an Angels game at Wrigley Field in LA. He invited me to come along and I jumped at the chance. Leon Jr. was so much older than me and it was kind of a neat relationship. He really looked after me and I kind of looked at him as an uncle. So he took me to the first game I ever saw in person.

The Angels started the 1939 season by winning 19 games in a row. The first game I ever saw was game number 20. The *LA Times* called the Angels the "Yankees of the West." I was excited to go see this undefeated team that everyone was talking about. The Angels promptly lost that game to the San Diego Padres 14-7.

My favorite professional team became the Hollywood Stars because they played at Gilmore Field which was only about a mile from my house. Gene Autry was one of their minority owners at the time. The guy who invented the Cobb salad, Bob Cobb, also owned the team.

My brother Leon took me to see the first baseball game that I ever attended

For a couple of years in the early 1940s, my best friend Sheldon Kaplan and I went to virtually every home game the

Stars played. We used to sneak in when they delivered the beer, hide under the stands until they opened the park, then we'd go sit down and watch the game. We'd stay after and get paid a penny apiece for picking up the seat cushions that they rented during the games. Sometimes we'd pick up as many as a hundred and fifty or two hundred seat cushions. And sometimes the clubhouse guy would let us come in and help shine shoes for a little bit of money. It was a lot of fun being around there. There was this pitcher name Cy Blanton who had been in the major leagues. I found a pouch of chewing tobacco in Cy's locker and tried it. I got as sick as could be. I could never keep from swallowing and I could never figure it out.

Anyway, that was a neat old ballpark, full of Hollywood personalities. Movie stars all over the place every night. But the games I remember more than anything else were on Sundays when my dad would take me. He was a life-long baseball fan. He loved the game. We'd go to a game and we didn't talk a lot. We'd just go and enjoy the game.

The Hollywood Stars were my favorite team when I was a kid. I grew up about a mile from Gilmore Field in Hollywood (newspaper clipping courtesy *Los Angeles Times*).

I loved the game so much and was so fascinated by it when I was a kid that I really became obsessed with it. My youngest sister Julie even helped me and one of my friends invent a game that I know would be popular with kids today. We took a card table and covered it with felt and drew a baseball diamond on it. For the players, we would put two screws coming up from the bottom of the table with a nut to keep them tight. Between the two screws was a rubber band, so that the player was like an inch wide. From center field down towards the mound, we took a curtain rod that had a track at the bottom of it and that's how you pitched. It was elevated in center field and the track came down to where the mound was. For the batter, we took a single faucet handle for the bat and that was anchored from underneath. Two people would play the game.

The pitcher would take a marble. By pressing down on his finger, he'd shoot it down the track and you could make it curve by pressing on one side or the other. The hitter would try to hit it with the faucet handle. If it hit one of the players, it was an out. With the rubber band under it, and if the ball got stuck, it was a double play if there was a man on. There were a couple of slats on the fence that was a double. If you happen to get it elevated and hit it over the fence, it was a home run.

My sister helped us build that – she was pretty artistic and she made advertising signs for the fence. It was really neat. At one point, we tried to patent the thing and it never got anywhere. We used to have tournaments and keep records and box scores. It was a pretty neat thing to do. We played that thing constantly. You could re-create it today and kids would love it. It would be way more fun than the hand-held games because you were actually doing it. It wasn't a computer telling you what happened.

It seemed like baseball kept crossing the paths of my life as a young person, or maybe it was the other way around.

In the late 1930s and early 1940s, there were three weekly and three monthly magazines. They used to employ kids to sell the magazines door-to-door and I used to sell all six publications. I think they sold for a nickel and we got a penny commission for selling them. You got Brownie Points for your sales and if you saved enough of them, you got a prize. There was one guy in my neighborhood that would buy whatever I was selling. I always had on a baseball cap and we'd talk a little bit of baseball or something.

One day in the winter, probably February 1941, when I went to his house the guy said to me, "Well, I won't be seeing you anymore. I'm leaving. I'm going to Spring Training."

I said, "What do you mean?"

He said, "I'm the third base coach for the New York Yankees."

His name was Art Fletcher, who had played shortstop for 13 seasons with the New York Giants and Philadelphia Phillies. He was also a Yankees coach for 19 seasons starting with the famous 1927 team.

Well, I thought it was pretty neat that I got to meet him. He asked for my address before he left, which I gave to him. About a month later I got a letter in the mail on hotel stationery from St. Petersburg with a little picture of him stuck up in the corner and autographs of the entire Yankees team. Forever I kept that letter in the envelope addressed to 337 North Mansfield with my name on it.

Art Fletcher

I finally sold it to a collector in Norfolk in 2007 because I didn't know what else to do with it. I also sold my autograph book. I had Connie Mack, Luke Appling, Al Simmons, Ted Lyons, and a number of other Hall of Famers. Now I regret like hell selling these things. I'd buy them back if he wanted to sell them.

But I digress again. I do that a lot when I'm telling stories.

Baseball was a big part of my life as a kid. In fact baseball has always been the primary thing in my life.

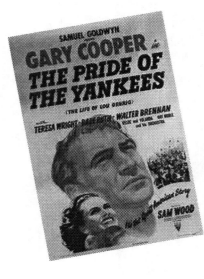

When I was 11 years old, they were casting for "Pride of the Yankees" at the MGM Studios. They were looking for someone to play the young Lou Gehrig. My mom was an actress and I thought what she did was really neat, so I thought I'd give it a shot. A couple or three of us friends went to the cattle call. There were probably five hundred kids overall. They had us throw a couple of balls and whatever else and they sent about four hundred of the kids home. They ended up narrowing the hundred finalists to a short list of about twenty and I made the cut. In fact, it got down to just two of us to play Lou Gehrig as a kid. I had to learn how to throw left-handed and the other kid was already left-handed, so he got the role. He happened to go to the same elementary school as me, Melrose Avenue Elementary School. His name was Douglas Croft, who is best remembered for being the first actor to portray Robin on television in the 1943 series "Batman."

I dabbled around a bit with theater when I was a kid. I kind of liked it and even majored in theater for a while when I was at UCLA. I was on a radio program called "The Hollywood Smarty Party" when I was around eight or 10 years old. It was a rip-off of a national radio show called "Quiz Kids" which was a very popular show. They had brilliant children on "Quiz Kids" and CBS radio in LA decided to copy it. Somehow I ended up on the show along with about four or five other kids. The emcee of the show was a man named Art Baker, who hosted numerous radio shows through the years. He also hosted shows when TV was in its infancy. Great voice. Little guy. He had this white shock of hair. He would ask questions that we'd try to answer for various prizes. I was on the show for ten or twelve weeks.

Art Baker

The funny thing about Art Baker was that he crossed my path again some fifteen years later. I was dating a girl named Faith Radenbaugh who was in the 1954 Miss Universe contest which was being held in Long Beach. After the contest ended, several of the girls went to perform an act at a nightclub in Hollywood called Earl Carroll's. The girls all wore bathing suits for one number, they sang behind people for another. They had their evening gowns on. Just looking really good. Anyway, I drove to pick her up at Earl Carroll's after her show was over. I was sitting at the bar waiting for her and who do I see at the other end of the bar? Yep … none other than Art Baker. I got up and walked down to the end of the bar. I tapped him on the shoulder and said, "Mr. Baker, you probably don't remember me."

Mr. Baker immediately looked at me and said, "Don't say anything." He looked me up and down and said, "I don't remember your name, but you're the kid from 'The Hollywood Smarty Party' who liked baseball."

The hair stood up on my neck. Unbelievable. The guy met eight zillion people in his life and he could make that connection from a little kid to a grown guy. Amazing.

I'll get back to Faith Radenbaugh later because that was a really interesting time in my life.

Dave Rosenfield
catcher

From my college yearbook

As a teenager, I liked playing a lot of sports. In addition to baseball, I played a little bit of basketball and football, but I was a midget. When I started the eleventh grade, I went out for lightweight football. I was five foot three and weighed one hundred and twenty pounds. I was so small and immature physically, I told people I was two years younger than I was because it appeared that way. As I said before, it wasn't until 2011 that I finally came clean about my real age. It really bothered me my whole life that I was lying about my age. I've really tried to base my life on being honest, and here's this lie I've been living with forever.

Anyway, I'd gotten a motor scooter in the fall of 1945 and I'd had it for one day. I had to take it in for some tune-up stuff and my dad took me to pick it up. I was riding to school and a woman ran a stop sign and hit me.

You know how you pop a paper bag? Well, I must have had a gas bubble. I got hit, went up in the air and landed flat on my back on the street and it popped an air bubble and blew up my intestine. It happened at nine in the morning and they finally did exploratory surgery on me at like one o'clock the next morning. My abdomen was absolutely rigid with peritonitis. They knew something was ruptured, but they didn't know what.

They said if it had happened just a few years earlier, I would have died. But now they had sulfa drugs and penicillin, which ultimately saved my life. It was bad enough that they had my brother flown home from the Army because they said I was going to die. I had a totally severed intestine.

I was totally out of it for a few days while I was in the hospital. When I came to, there was a nurse in my hospital room and the first words out of my mouth were, "Who won the World Series?" It was the last day of the last game of the World Series between the Tigers and Cubs. The nurse said she didn't know who had won the series and she left to go ask someone. By the time she came back to the room, I was out again and I didn't wake up for like another day later. It's one of those parts of your life that is just obliterated because I do not remember anything other than I know for a fact that the Cubs didn't win. And it just so happens that it was the last time the Cubs were in the World Series.

That accident ended my football career. By the next year, I was six feet, about one hundred seventy five pounds. I grew nine inches in a year. They thought the car accident might have had something to do with the growth spurt, but they didn't know for sure. The growth spurt enabled me to become a better baseball player, even though I'd lost a lot of coordination. I played ball whenever I could. I grew up playing for my teams at John Burroughs Junior High and Los Angeles High School. I also played semi pro at Dorsey High and on fields all over the LA area.

A number of the big bands of the day, for fun, had baseball teams. They would play each other and they would come and play us at the playground. One of the bands was Freddy Martin who was very well known and played at the Coconut Grove at the Ambassador Hotel in Los Angeles. His vocalist was Merv Griffin, who went on to do great things in television. The Harry James Band, probably one of the biggest bands of the day, not only had a team, but Harry James played on the team. We were playing the Harry James Band in a playground game and I was playing third base. Harry James slid into third and broke his leg. It was one of the loudest noises I have ever heard. Betty Grable, James' wife and also the pin-up queen of the world at the time, was in the stands and came running down to the field. We were all standing there watching him writhing in agony and Betty Grable was right there with us looking at her husband.

Jackie Robinson

Our semi-pro team once played against Jackie Robinson when he played for the Los Angeles Police Department's team. I knew that he was a great athlete because he starred in four sports at UCLA when my sister Jo was the editor of the UCLA student newspaper, the *Daily Bruin*. I had no idea that he'd be the guy to go on to break the color barrier in the Major Leagues just a few years later.

I played on the same playground team as Billy Consolo and Sparky Anderson and a bunch of other guys. They used to call me "Rabbit" because I had big ears. Anyway, I remained close with Sparky forever.

I digress from my youth for a minute.

The Norfolk Sports Club, an organization supporting athletics in the Hampton Roads area, hosts an annual dinner called the "Jamboree" during which they award several scholarships to local athletes. A big-name speaker entertains the crowd of 600-1000 people. One year in the early 1970s, the organizers of the dinner asked me if I knew Sparky, who was managing the Cincinnati Reds at the time. They asked me if could get him to speak at the Jamboree.

I went to the Winter Meetings and ran in to Sparky and told him about the dinner and how much they wanted him to be their featured speaker. I told him he could set his own date. Sparky told me he'd be happy to do it.

I said to him, "Aren't you going to ask me how much money they're going to pay you for speaking?"

"No."

"Really?"

"I'm not doing it for the money. I'm doing it because you asked me to."

He came to Norfolk and spoke at the dinner, which was a huge success. He was paid five or ten thousand dollars. The next day after he spoke, I went to breakfast with him and then was going to take him to the airport. He held out the check and said, "Isn't this the greatest thing in the world?"

I said, "What do you mean?"

He said, "Up until like a year or two ago, I had to work all winter to make this much money. I got up and just told stories for 20 minutes and they give me all this money. Isn't this the greatest thing in the world?"

He was a terrific guy. He never changed, even with all his success. He was just a simple ol' guy. He had a good-looking sister. I used to tell him that I hated when his sister used to come to our games because I'd spend the entire game looking up into the stands.

Anyway, I guess I was a good enough high school catcher to earn baseball scholarship offers in 1947 to the University of Southern California, UCLA and Cal Poly San Luis Obispo. I really wanted to go away to school at that time. Southern Cal was a big baseball school. There was this guy named John Albini who was the All-City catcher and he was going to Southern Cal. So their coach Rod Dedeaux suggested I change positions. I told Dedeaux, "I don't want to change positions. If I'm going to play pro ball, it's going to have to be as a catcher."

So I didn't go to USC.

I was the editor of the *Los Angeles Times* on "Kid's Day" in 1947. That's me in the middle with my head cocked and my big ears.

I knew three guys from high school who were going to UCLA, but Cal Poly sounded good to me. I was all set to go to San Luis Obispo, and about two weeks before I was to leave, I got a call. The Veterans Administration had cut some of Cal Poly's funds, so they were going to have to abridge my scholarship to half of what they had offered. My family didn't have any money at this time. The scholarship was not going to cover my living expenses. I couldn't afford to go to Cal Poly. I could, however, afford to go to UCLA and live at home, so I switched and went to UCLA. Incidentally, part of my scholarship included ten tickets to UCLA football games that we could do whatever we wanted with. We were even allowed to sell them, and I'd get five dollars apiece for them.

While I was at UCLA, students were required at that time to take a course in boxing, wrestling, or fencing. I took boxing in the afternoon but I was never there because of baseball. The coach told me that I had to have at least one fight. So I fought somebody under 170 pounds. He was pretty good. I wasn't. There were three one-minute rounds, which sounds very short until you try doing it. I wasn't smart enough just to take a couple of punches and go down. And this guy almost killed me. The coach couldn't stop laughing. He was handling the bell, and I know some of those rounds went more than one minute. He broke my nose and knocked me down I don't know how many times. He nearly beat me to death. I kept thinking those one-minute rounds were never going to end.

While at UCLA, I became friendly with many of the athletes who were attending school and playing sports. One of the basketball players I knew was a backup forward on one of John Wooden's first teams at UCLA. His given name was Krekor Ohanian, but due to the discrimination he endured as a member of the Armenian community, he changed his name to Mike Connors. Due to his prowess playing good defense on the basketball court, he became known as "Touch" Connors. But he became better known because he played the title role in the hit CBS television series "Mannix."

The theater program at UCLA was a pretty big deal back then. There were many, many people who went on to have wonderful careers in the entertainment business after studying theater at UCLA. I decided to major in theater for a short period when I was there before I switched to something else. In one of the introductory classes, we were in a huge auditorium style classroom. I was working for the *LA Times* at the time, getting about two hours of sleep a night. I was going to school and playing ball. I had a lot going on. I was sitting about two-thirds the way up in this classroom and I fell asleep. I woke up because the professor was standing over me with a rolled up newspaper, beating on me. "You will not sleep in my class!" He was just screaming at me and beating on me. There were probably a hundred-some people in there just laughing at me. I was horribly embarrassed. I wonder now if I was the one who delivered his copy of the *Times* to him.

Art Reichle, UCLA's head baseball coach for thirty years starting in the 1940s, had made all kinds of promises to me. He was going to get me a campus job. Tuition and books meant very little because they were so cheap. My first semester at UCLA, tuition was only $29. My books were like $30. I was working for the *Times* delivering papers from the time I was eleven or twelve years old. I made pretty good money; that way I could do other things and play ball. So I needed to work. I was supposed to get a campus job. Reichle kept promising me and never came up with it. I played freshman baseball in 1948, and I was going to be the backup catcher on the varsity the next year. But I still hadn't gotten the campus job. I kept going to Reichle and I kept saying, "Coach, if I don't get this campus job, I'm leaving."

Reichle said, "What do you mean you're *leaving*?"

I said, "I'm going to transfer."

"Where can *you* go?" Reichle asked.

"I don't know. I can go *someplace* and play."

"Well, you can't go anywhere. You'll have to sit out a year," Reichle said to me.

I said, "No. No I don't. I will go to a junior college." Transfers to junior colleges were not bound by the same rule as the NCAA.

Reichle said to me, "*Nobody* in their right mind would transfer from UCLA to go to a junior college."

I said, "Well, *I* will. I've got to have the job."

Reichle told me again, "I think I've got something for you."

I told him, "No. I'm out of here."

And with that, I left UCLA and went to Los Angeles City College and started playing baseball there. All these schools played each other all the time and there was this one day when we happened to be playing UCLA. Art Reichle just stared into our dugout and glared at me the whole time. He was riding me the whole game. I thought that was the most chicken shit thing in history. He was kind of a legendary coach and to be riding a kid was really bad I thought.

So I played ball at L.A. City College. And I was going to school, but didn't really know *why* I was going to school. All I wanted to do was play ball. So I said to my dad, "How about letting me go play pro ball?"

Pop said, "No. I want you to finish college."

I said, "I don't know what I'm doing. I'm changing majors every semester. I really don't know why I'm going to school. If I promise to finish college, will you let me go play?"

Pop said, "If you promise me."

I said, "You've got my word."

CHAPTER FOUR

GIVING IT A SHOT

There were baseball scouts all over southern California. I knew a lot of those guys because they were always around our games. I played everywhere and it seemed like these scouts were just always around looking to sign players for their minor league teams. I was a pretty good catcher with a great arm. I was a pretty good hitter but had no power. I had people trying to sign me for a while. The St. Louis Browns tried signing me in high school and they were going to send me to Big Stone Gap, Virginia. Obviously, I passed.

In fact, I was even looked at one time by a legendary scout named Howie Haak. He was considered one of the top scouts in the world because he was bilingual and could go into Latin America to look at players. He was with the Dodgers and then went to the Pirates and is widely credited with stealing Roberto Clemente from Brooklyn and bringing him to Pittsburgh. In my post-playing days, I told Howie, "People always say what a great scout you are. Well I don't think that you are a very good scout."

He said, *"Really? Why not?"*

I said, "Because you tried to sign *me!*"

I ended up signing a contract with the Philadelphia Phillies in 1950. The guy who signed me was a guy named Danny Regan. He would later play a role in my career as a front office executive.

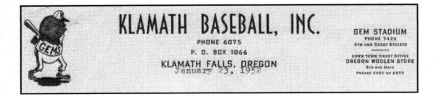

Anyway, I travelled to Lodi for Spring Training. I was supposed to be assigned to the Class D Klamath Falls Gems, a team in the Far West League, the lowest rung on the professional baseball ladder. Hub Kittle, whose baseball career as a player, coach and executive spanned 68 years, was the manager of the Gems.

The regular catcher for Klamath Falls was George Triandos, brother of longtime Baltimore Orioles catcher Gus Triandos. George subsequently had a stellar 1950 season, leading the Far West League with 183 base hits and ranking twelfth in the circuit with a .347 batting average.

I was fighting a kid named Dan Linton for the backup job for the Klamath Falls team and they opted for him. He was a left-handed hitter, which was partially why they chose him. And ... they may have thought he was *better* than I was.

Hub Kittle called me into his office and told me they were going to send me to Americus, Georgia to another Class D team in the Georgia-Florida League. I said, "You're going to send me where? I understand it's in Georgia, but where in the hell...?" My problem was that I didn't have transportation home guaranteed in my contract.

In those days, players had to negotiate their transportation home when the season was over. I signed for $150 a month and even if I'd played all year I couldn't save enough to get home. I told Kittle, "If I go down there and they release me, I don't have enough money to get home on."

Kittle said, "I understand, but that's what the Phillies want to do."

I said, "I can't afford to go there unless you can get them to guarantee me transportation home."

"Dave, I tried, but they won't," Kittle said. I told Hub that I couldn't go. He said, "Okay. I like you. You go home, but you know the rules say that I'm going to have to suspend you. You go home, wait there and I'll get you a job."

Hub Kittle

So I went home to Los Angeles for about four days when Kittle called and asked me how fast I could get to Stockton. I said, "I don't know. How fast is the train? I can leave today or tomorrow."

"I got you a job in Stockton." This coach came through on his promise, unlike Art Reichle.

Kittle told me to call the Stockton Ports General Manager, Dave Kelly. Stockton operated in the Class C

California League as an independent team without a full working agreement with a Major League club. Some Major League teams, such as the St. Louis Browns, had agreed to send a few players to Stockton and the rest of the roster would be filled with players whose contracts were not property of any big league organization.

I signed a contract with Stockton for $175 a month, but I hardly played at all. I had very few plate appearances. So Kelly called me in and said they were going to send me to Eugene to give me a chance to play. Stockton had a partial working agreement with the Browns and they had sent in some guy who was going to play ahead of me. By now I was looking around and 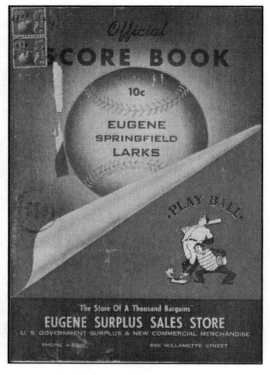 I saw guys that were better than I was and I start to understand that I was probably not going to be a Major League catcher. This would be very important to me because I did not spend years and years being a minor league player. I knew I had wanted to do something better with my life than be a minor league baseball player. I got it out of my system.

So I went to Eugene to join another Class D Far West League team, the Eugene Larks. I joined the team on the road. Rosters in those days were sixteen or seventeen maximum. We had like twenty eight guys on this team, and every day twelve guys would be on some kind of inactive list. Tomorrow you might play and then you'd be on some other list. So I stayed there for about two weeks, again I didn't play a lot. The ball club was in complete disarray. The manager had been suspended for some reason and a guy who was the general manager at a lumber mill owned by the team's owner was brought in to run the team. He didn't even know half the guys' names. I looked around and said to myself, "This isn't getting me anywhere. I promised my dad I would go back to school, so I'm going back to school."

And that's exactly what I did.

CHAPTER FIVE

IN THE NAVY

The Korean War was going on and Cal State Los Angeles (also referred to as LA State) had just started a baseball program. It was an upper division school and you had to have upper division status to get in. It was on the campus with LA City College. All these schools had guys who had played a little bit of pro ball. Nobody paid any attention to it. So I played on the first team that LA State fielded.

It was now the fall of 1951 and I was about to get drafted into the Army. The Korean War was not a war anyone wanted to be in. It was not a popular war. Nobody wanted to go into the Army. We knew we were going to have to serve, but we wanted to serve the best we could without having to go to Korea.

A bunch of us hung out at a hot dog stand right next to the campus. After class, I went to the hot dog stand and was playing cards with three of my friends. All of a sudden, these guys got up and said they had to go.

I said, "Where are you going?"

They said, "We've got to go to the base."

I said, "What do you mean you have to go to the base?"

"Well, we just went into the Navy," they said.

"What do you mean you went into the Navy?"

"We were about to get drafted into the Army but we got a deal where we'd go into the Navy and play basketball," my friends said.

This was very interesting to me. I wanted to know more about what they were talking about. Basically, here's what happened ...

George Yardley, who would ultimately become the first player in NBA history to score 2,000 points in a single season en route to a Hall of Fame NBA career with the Ft. Wayne/Detroit Pistons, was about to get drafted into the Army. Yardley's father was friends with the commanding officer of the Los Alamitos Naval Air Station in Orange County. The two knew each other from the Newport Beach Yacht Club. The commanding officer said, "We can't have him go into the Army. We'll get him into the Navy and we'll put together a basketball team at Los Alamitos."

George Yardley

The Los Alamitos Naval Air Station had weekend reserve squadrons, but the squadrons were all at half strength. Nobody ever heard of Los Alamitos. I played ball all over southern California and I had never heard of it. They wanted to do something to elevate the profile of the base and they thought that having good sports teams would increase their publicity and get the squadrons up to strength. Word spread about the commander's desire to build a strong athletic program, and my friends – Al Roges, Hal Uplinger and Roland Hans – all decided to play basketball in the Navy rather than get drafted into the Army.

All three guys had played basketball briefly at Long Island University during the New York City point-shaving scandal during the early 1950s. Several college basketball players were prosecuted for their roles in the gambling racket, but not my friends. Roges left LIU when they wouldn't cut him in on the fix. Uplinger stayed at LIU and never knew what the hell was going on. Roges used to say, "Uppy could never figure it out. He'd be open under the basket screaming for the ball and nobody would throw it to him. He couldn't ever figure out why they wouldn't give him the ball."

After his stint in the Navy, Uplinger spent the 1953-54 season in the NBA with the Baltimore Bullets. He got into the television business and became one of the early producers of NFL telecasts for CBS. In 1985, he produced the American side of "Live Aid" and was responsible for the international distribution of the 16-hour broadcast to 155 countries that raised $127 million for the Band Aid Trust.

The Navy basketball team at Los Alamitos also included Johnny Arndt and Don Eby. Arndt later became the longtime athletic director at Loyola University in LA and Eby played at USC.

It was because of George Yardley that these guys all went into the Navy.

But I digress.

I asked these guys if they thought the Los Alamitos base would be interested in having a baseball team in addition to the basketball team. They suggested I go down there myself and ask them. So the next day, I went to the base to talk to them about it. They asked me if I thought I could get some guys. I said I knew a lot of guys who were about to get drafted. They said if I could I could put together a team, they'd love to do it. So I went into the United States Navy and got involved with the start up of the baseball team.

I was involved with the purchasing of equipment, scheduling and publicity. We took care of the baseball fields and the gymnasium. All of the athletes in the Navy were required to have jobs during their off-seasons. We used to have to stand night watches. We had a bunch of nut cases. When we started, we were standing night watches on the flight line and the perimeter of the base with rifles. Some of these guys are out there shooting rabbits in the middle of the goddamn night, so they said no more weapons for us. We now had to stand guard with a freakin' billy stick! If somebody was going to do something, what was I going to do with a billy stick?

Some of the guys decided to have some fun with George Yardley. He was pretty naïve. One night he's standing guard on the flight line. Some of the guys put on these ski masks, they came out and grabbed him and said they were going to steal an airplane.

Yardley said, "I can't let you do that."

The guys said, "Well, we're gonna. And if you don't let us, we'll kill you."

"What do you want me to do?" Yardley said.

"We need your help," the guys said.

One of the guys got into the cockpit. They made George pull the propeller through to get him to start the engine. And they just let him stand out there endlessly. When he finally figured it out, I thought he was going to kill somebody.

All branches of the military fielded various athletic teams that competed not only against one another, but against local semi-pro, AAU and college teams, and the baseball teams even competed against professional clubs during Spring Training in their respective areas. The service teams would ultimately play in tournaments to declare national champions in their respective sports.

Our basketball team was tremendous. This was a base of only approximately six hundred and fifty men, and we won the Service Championship of the World in four sports - baseball, basketball, volleyball and water polo. We had five or six guys on the Olympic water polo team in 1952. We had several guys on the Olympic track team in '52. Our basketball team beat the National AAU Champion Peoria Caterpillars. We had a lot of our basketball players on the volleyball team – that's how good that was.

Don Eby was a complete character. He and I went out one night and drank everything that stood still. We ended up with two gals in Newport Beach. Neither one of us knew what the hell had happened. These two girls took us home to their house. We woke up in the morning and the girls were gone. The two of us were there in this house. It was about ten thirty or eleven in the morning. We were supposed to be at the base at eight o'clock. We were both in a panic. Eby kept saying we were going to get court martialed because we were AWOL.

I was still half in the bag. I said, "Let me think. We aren't going to go to the base at all."

He said, "What do you mean we aren't going to the base?"

I said, "I'm going to think of something. The worst thing we can do right now is show up now. By the time we get anywhere, it's going to be one or two o'clock in the afternoon. The worst thing we can do is show up today."

I finally said, "Okay. I've got a plan. We'll go tomorrow morning and be there at eight. We'll just act like nothing's wrong."

So we went to the base the next day and got there around a quarter of eight. They stopped us at the gate and arrested us because we were reported AWOL. I said to the shore patrol guy, "What the hell are you guys talking about? We aren't AWOL. We had the day off yesterday."

The patrol guy said, "Who gave you the day off?"

I said, "The guy we work for, Bill Marunda."

The guy said, "*Huh?* He's the guy who reported you AWOL."

I said, "Well, he gave us the day off. We had done so well with our project the day before."

So they handcuffed us, put us in the goddamn paddy wagon and they drove us to go see Marunda. He had been in the Navy for like 20-some years and was still first-class and had never made chief. They marched us in to see him with guns and everything. I kept telling Eby to keep a straight face. Marunda said, "You caught 'em!"

I said, "What is the story here? You gave us the day off!"

He said, "*I did?*"

I said, "You told us what a great job we did the other day and you told us we could have the day off."

"*I did?*"

"Absolutely!"

"Oh. Okay guys, let 'em go."

But I digress.

I was on the baseball team in 1952. One day we had to play a double header in Inyo-Kern at a naval weapons station. It felt like it was 400 degrees out there in the middle of the Mohave Desert. Something was wrong with our regular catcher and I ended up having to catch both games. I wasn't very big then; I played at about 170 pounds. I think I lost 25 pounds that day. When the day was over, I could hardly walk. I ended up taking a stool and put it in the shower. We got a case of beer and two or three of us just sat in the shower and drank beer. I must have sat in there for like 30 or 40 minutes just to get some fluids back in me. I was lucky I didn't pass out or die.

Anyhow, we went to the National Semi-Pro tournament in Wichita, and we were going to play the opening game. Dizzy Dean, who was broadcasting the "Game of the Day" on the radio, was doing our game. The night before the first game, a guy from Camp Rucker, Alabama and I went to dinner with Dizzy Dean to give him the dope about the teams and all that. (Incidentally, Dizzy Dean played in the 1938 World Series for the Chicago Cubs – the same series that introduced me to Major League Baseball.)

Our team did so well at the Wichita tournament that the next year, we played in the 11th Naval District Major League and played 140 games against teams from the San Diego

Naval Station, the Marine Recruit Depot, Camp Pendleton Marine Base, Amphibious Base Pacific, El Toro Marine Base and colleges from all over southern California. In the spring, we'd play against professional teams training nearby, including the Los Angeles Angels.

In 1953, the second year of the Los Alamitos Naval Air Station baseball program, we wanted to go back to Wichita to play in the same tournament we'd been successful at the previous year. The first year, there were 32 teams in the tournament and 31 of them were service teams. Everybody in the world was in the service. Willie Mays was there. Dick Groat. Everyone was in the Navy or Army.

They had revived the Inter-Service World Series in 1953. But the admiral of the 11th Naval District said, "You're not going back to Wichita. We want you to play for the Navy Championship. And if you win that, we want you to go on to the Service Series." We asked if we go could go to Wichita if we didn't win and he said "Maybe." So we played in some tournament with teams from Hawaii, northern California and somewhere else. We won that. Then we went to Jacksonville to play for the Navy Championship. We played a team from Little Creek Amphibious Base in Virginia Beach, and won that. Then we went to Quantico to play in the Inter-Service World Series against the Marines, Air Force and Army and won that. We were the Service Champions of the World.

It was funny because when we flew to Jacksonville, we flew in an old beat-up plane and we couldn't take a lot of our gear because the plane couldn't carry the load. All we had were our dress blues and fatigues. It was hotter than hell in August in Jacksonville, and all we had were these heavy goddamned uniforms. Every other place in the world was wearing whites. Whites were never the uniform of the day in the 11th Naval District at that time. So we sat in the barracks playing cards and drinking beer between going out to play. It rained every day. It was just awful.

We got to Quantico and we had a lieutenant commander named Doss Donohoe who travelled with us and was our officer in charge. I was the ranking guy on the ball club at that time, because I had my three little green stripes a couple weeks longer than some other guy. This lieutenant commander was a great guy. He really liked us. He was a very superstitious person. He always sat on the ball bag. We had two completely different factions on the team – a bunch of us who smoked and drank and had a good time and a bunch of guys we called "milkshake drinkers." The commander liked going with us and hanging out with us. So he said to five or six of us that he wanted to take us to dinner that night. We were in civilian clothes and he took us to the Officer's Club. The Marine General, who had been at the ball game, recognized some of us, and I thought that poor commander was going to the brig or something for bringing us in there. The General knew we were all enlisted people. We were told to leave. So we did.

The next day was the finals and we won the Inter-Service World Series. So now, the Admiral in charge of the 11th Naval District sent a Super Constellation – the finest airplane of the day – to bring us back to California. The Super Constellation was so nice that President Dwight D. Eisenhower used this type of plane as his presidential aircraft. We went back in style. We learned that winning was important.

I'm receiving a trophy during the awards ceremony after our
team won the Service Championship of the World in 1953

During the early 1950s, my family went through some
tough times. My dad died in 1951. My second-oldest sister,
Louise, was fighting cancer just a year later. My mom flew
to New Jersey to be with her. Knowing how grave Louise's
situation was, I did all I could to see my sister one final time.
I tried to catch hops on Navy planes from California. To get
there took four or five flights. One flight wasn't pressurized
and I had a cold and developed a terrible ear infection. By
the time I got to New Jersey, I was in excruciating pain. I got
there after the funeral.

I was in terrible pain and started losing my hearing
completely. They took me to Fort Dix Army Hospital in
central New Jersey. I was in the hospital for more than two
weeks. For a good portion of that time, I was stone deaf. I
caught a lot of shit being the only sailor in this Army
hospital. They would mouth things to me, knowing I

couldn't hear. Guys are terrible anyways. There was this one guy who had just been circumcised and the guys would get a newspaper and slip in a picture of a nude girl and give it to him. You'd hear him screaming. Anyway, my infection eventually cleared up and I got my hearing back.

But I digress.

Baseball certainly played a key role in my service days and enabled me to travel a lot. Our team went to play in a state semi-pro tournament in San Luis Obispo. At the evening meal one night, the only thing they had to eat was liver. Well, you already know that I didn't eat liver. The other guys didn't either. So I said, "Let's go into town to get something to eat."

We hitchhiked into town and we went into this bar. We started having some beers. They finally swept us out of there at like 2:00 am or something. We hitched a ride back to Camp Roberts. It was pretty deserted and we were all hungry because we forgot to get something to eat. Well, there was no place open at that time of night. We were staying in these little huts, like four beds to a hut. So we were walking down this street in the camp and we saw this commissary. We thought they'd have something to eat in there.

It was pretty deserted around there but we didn't care. Everything was locked up. We climbed in through a window that we pried open. We got into the kitchen and turned some lights on. They had these big giant refrigerators. The only thing we could find that was any good were these giant meatloaves. Army meatloaf was about two feet long and about as thick as a football. So, we each took a meatloaf and went walking down the company street. We got back to our hut and ate whatever we wanted and went to bed.

We woke up in the morning and Commander Donohoe was standing in the middle of our little hut. He said, "Do any of you guys know anything about anybody breaking into the commissary?"

I said, "You *asking* us?"

Commander Donohoe said, "Well, *somebody* broke in during the middle of the night last night."

I said, "We went to town last night. We don't know anything about that."

Donohoe kept saying, "You sure you don't know anything about that?"

"Yes sir. Not us." And he's standing right by my bed.

"Rosenfield, *are you sure?*"

I said, "Yes, sir!"

Commander Donohoe began pointing. I had taken my meatloaf and it was standing up in my shoe. *There's a two-foot long meatloaf standing up in my shoe!* Talk about getting caught with the goods! Donohoe just started laughing. I didn't get in trouble. He covered for us.

There was a lot of covering for each other in the Navy; having each other's backs was such an important element of teamwork. Even though there were a lot of guys with culturally diverse backgrounds, we were still on the same team. Our ethnicity, religion, or skin color didn't matter – everyone was called names and everyone was teased. We were just friends and we were very tight. Nobody thought twice about possibly being offended by a nickname called by someone else in our group.

At this same tournament in San Luis Obispo, there was some guy sitting behind our bench, just riding us all game long for no apparent reason. Just screaming and yelling at people. The game was over, we were walking back to the base and this guy started following us out of the ballpark, calling us "stupid swabbies" and stuff like that. It was really aggravating. I turned around and said we'd had enough of his crap. I told him, "Go home and beat your wife."

This guy shouted back, "Shut up Jew! If I want something out of you, I'll kick it out of you." Next thing I knew I had this guy on the ground and I was going to kill him. I was beating the absolute crap out of him. My friends pulled me off and said, "What the hell is wrong with you?"

I said, "Did you hear what he called me?"

They said, "Yeah, but we call you that all the time."

I said, "*You* can, that's okay. I don't care. But I'm not letting someone *who's not one of us* talk to us that way."

That was one of the few physical altercations I was ever involved in.

But I digress.

I mentioned earlier about the fact we had to work jobs during our off-season. Somebody told me the fire department was a great gig. On 24 hours, off 24, on 24, off 48. You didn't do anything. It's a great, great deal. So I applied for the fire department. Well, I was scared to death of heights. Sliding down a fire pole terrified me. I used to run down the steps. Stepping off into space and grabbing a pole was all I could do.

We never did anything. We dragged hoses around, but we didn't do much. So all of a sudden, they called us together one day and said that we were going to begin training on burning airplanes. So we crawled into a burning airplane wearing asbestos suits and had to pull a dummy out of this airplane. Well, I did it. It scared me to death, but I did it.

We played around with that for a few days. Then they said we were going to move on to structural fires. Well, I had never noticed they had a fire tower, like four stories high, with a ladder all the way to the top. You had to go up the ladder dragging a fire hose. I looked at this thing saying, "There's no way in the world that I can do that!" So I kept going to the back of the line.

The chief says, "Rosenfield, I haven't seen you go up yet."

I said, "No sir."

The chief said, "You've got to go."

I said, "No sir."

"What do you mean, 'No sir'?"

I said, "I can't do that."

"It's a direct order."

"I can't do that."

Fed up at this point, the chief asked me, "Well, why not?"

I said, "Because I'll die."

"Why?"

"I'll either have a heart attack or I'll fall. There's no question in my mind."

The chief said, "This is a direct order! You're going up there!"

I said, "Sir, may I ask a question?"

"Yes."

At this point, everyone was standing around laughing. I said, "If I don't go up there, are you going to shoot me?"

"No."

"Well, then I'm not going."

The chief said, "I'm going to have to put you on report. You're going to have to stand a captain's mast." No one in their right might wanted to go through that process. It was like a punishment hearing.

I said, "Sir, you've got to do what you've got to do. With all due respect, I can't do that."

The chief was trying not to laugh and he didn't know what the hell to make of it. So he put me on report and now I had to stand a captain's mast. The commanding officer knew me quite well. He used to be at all our ball games. He was trying like hell not to laugh. The fire chief, this officer who reported me, was not too thrilled because he was looking pretty foolish.

The commanding officer said, "Mr. Rosenfield, I'm going to have to discipline you."

And with that, I was confined to quarters for like 24 hours or something. And that was the end of that.

My two-year stint in the Navy ended in 1954 with plenty of memories and stories. But when I got out, I had some unfinished business to attend to. I told my father I would finish school. I went to see a counselor at Cal State LA and said, "I need you to look at my record and tell me what I'm closest to a degree in."

When in school prior to going into the Navy to play ball, I changed majors like every ten minutes. I'd been a theater major, a speech major, math major, journalism major and something else. I didn't care what I was going to get my degree in; I just wanted to get out.

I was still playing baseball. In fact, I caught for Don Drysdale when he got out of high school for a couple of games. He wasn't very good because he threw from over the top. Once he signed with the Dodgers, they dropped his arm angle and that made all the difference.

We played games all over because LA State didn't have their own field. We played in Burbank, at Griffith Park, in Huntington Park and in Chavez Ravine. We played mostly in Chavez Ravine during my last year on the same site where Dodger Stadium would be built a few years later.

One day, we were playing a double header against San Diego State. A guy named Art Preston, who ended up becoming a running back for the Chicago Bears, hit a home run in the first inning. I was standing at home plate as he rounded the bases. I had my mask in my right hand and my catcher's mitt on my left. Preston crossed the plate and for no apparent reason, he hit me with a forearm across my nose. I was bleeding all over the place and lying on the ground in agony. He broke my nose, and to this day, I still don't know why. I have no idea if my teammates went after him or what happened because I was down and nearly out. They took me in the dugout and they started to fix my nose, packing it with whatever they could to stop the bleeding. All of a sudden, I looked up and my mother was in the dugout. I was as embarrassed as I have been in my whole life. I screamed at her, "Would you get the hell out of here!" I ended up catching both games with this shit in my nose. I couldn't breath.

But I digress.

The counselor reviewed my academic record and discovered that many of my previous courses would qualify me for a degree in Language Arts. He said, "If you take everything we tell you to take, you can get out in two years."

I said, "Sign me up right now."

My journey through college, which treated me to a career playing professional baseball, a stint in the United States Navy and even a year working for my sister in Daytona Beach, ended in January 1956 with a degree in Language Arts from Cal State Los Angeles. Eight and a half years had passed since I graduated from high school, and it was five years since my father passed away.

But I kept my promise to Pop.

CHAPTER SIX

MY STAR-CROSSED LIFE

I've always had a lot of very interesting people who I have been associated with. I find people to be very intriguing. Growing up in Los Angeles, I was fortunate to know some people who became pretty popular both in the sports world and in the entertainment business. You already know about Jackie Robinson and Sparky Anderson. There were Harry James and Art Baker. I scared the crap out of John Carradine and sold magazines to a Yankees coach. My life just kind of weaved in and around and I found myself knowing these people, usually before they went on to become famous.

One such person was David Janssen. When I was in the ninth grade at John Burroughs Junior High, David Janssen was in the seventh grade. A friend of mine and I coached the seventh grade baseball team. David Janssen was our pitcher. He was a very nice kid. He went on to be a good basketball player and pole-vaulter at Fairfax High. He ended up as a well-known Hollywood actor and played the main character in the television series "The Fugitive."

David Janssen

When I was a senior at LA High School in 1947, there were two graduating classes. There was the "Senior A" class that graduated in June and the "Senior B" class that graduated in January. The two classes together formed the Star & Crescent Society and I was elected as president. One of my jobs was to line up the entertainment for some show.

Kay Starr was a very popular singer at the time. In fact, she was one of the top performers of the day. I don't recall how I did this, but I somehow got Kay Starr to come and perform at this show. People thought it was pretty neat that I was able to get Kay Starr to come to our school.

Kay Starr

As a teenager and probably even into my twenties, I was probably too interested in playing sports to really become consumed with girls and dating and that whole thing. I dated girls here and there, but usually it wasn't too serious. One of my teammates was dating this one girl who came to our Sunday games. I couldn't stop staring at her. She was absolutely gorgeous. Well, I kind of stole her from him and we started dating for a while.

Her name was Suzan Ball – she was Lucille Ball's second cousin. Suzan was also direct descendant of the Mayflower's John Alden, who is said to have been the first person to set foot on Plymouth Rock in 1620. We dated for a while but I was way out of my league with her. Suzan was named one of the most important new stars of 1953. She ended up getting married to actor Richard Long in 1954 and Tony Curtis, Rock Hudson, Janet Leigh and David Janssen were in attendance at her wedding. She was said to have fallen in love with a married Anthony Quinn during the filming of "City Beneath the Sea" in 1953. Unfortunately, she died of cancer at the tender age of 21.

A studio photo of Suzan Ball

I also became pretty good friends in college with Billy Barty. Billy Barty was one of the most well-known "little people" in America thanks to roles in many movies and television shows. He was perhaps best known for his part in the Peter Gunn television show and for being in the Spike Jones Band. Billy was a remarkable athlete. He was about three feet four inches, but man could he play golf! He'd hit the ball as straight as could be. He played basketball a little bit and would drive people crazy because he was under their feet all the time. At LA City College, he even got into a football game against the Southern Cal freshmen.

Billy Barty in the LA City College football team photo

My friends and I used to go out on the town quite often with Billy. He could sing. He could dance. We'd go into a bar and we'd take Billy and put him up on the piano or put him up on the bar and he'd end up entertaining. He really was a lot of fun.

One night, Billy and I went out and met some girls. We were all getting along pretty well and we decided we were going to go someplace. The girls had a nice car. I didn't. And Billy's car was adapted for him, with extended pedals so he could work the gas, the brake and everything else. One of the girls drove her car. We decided we were going to go to the beach. We go someplace and have a drink and then we start home. And I'm in the back seat with this girl trying to make points and I'm not paying much attention to the front seat. I look up, Billy's girl is driving and Billy is standing on the seat, almost mugging her, kissing her on the neck and on the ear. It was one of the funniest things I'd ever seen. The girl I was with and I couldn't stop laughing. So that was kind of the end of that date. Billy was great with full-sized women. They thought he was so cute, that he was a little toy guy. Then they'd find out that he wasn't kidding around.

In 1954, I was dating a gal named Faith Radenbaugh, who I referred to earlier when I was telling the story of meeting Art Baker again 15 years after being on the "Hollywood Smarty Party." She was Miss Wyoming, but had never been in Wyoming in her life. She knew a guy who bought the rights to several states for beauty pageants. A couple of the pageants he didn't want to put on, so he would just name somebody as "Miss Whatever State." So he named her Miss Wyoming. We had to find someone with an address who would claim to be an aunt or something. I groped around and found a place called Heart Mountain, Wyoming and found a woman who agreed to be her aunt.

I came halfway close to marrying her, but it was a very difficult situation. Her folks were violently anti-Semitic.

They couldn't stand her being anywhere around me. I can remember going to the door and having her mom yell, "Faith, *the Jew's here!*" That bothered me because I cared about her and I knew how difficult it would be for that relationship to go anywhere. You can't make people like who they don't like.

I felt so strongly about Faith that I argued with my mother to the point that our relationship became estranged for a period of time. I thought my mom overstepped her bounds by calling Faith's parents to complain about their anti-Semitism. My mother was incensed that I had given Faith a ring that had been in our family for years. It wasn't an engagement ring or anything like that, but my mother didn't like that I had given it to her when her parents were so awful. I just couldn't tolerate it. So I made up my mind that I was leaving and I moved to Florida to stay with my sister when she worked on the newspaper in Daytona Beach. My mother and I didn't speak for nearly two years. That was the loneliest time of my life, especially around family gatherings and holidays. My brother got my mother and me ultimately to apologize to each other.

When it was time for me to move back to LA, I ran an ad in the Daytona newspaper asking if anyone wanted to share a ride to California to help me share expenses. I never got any response. About a day and a half before I was supposed to leave, I got a phone call from a woman asking if I could go by way of Las Vegas. She asked if I'd consider taking a dog to Las Vegas. Her family was moving to Vegas and they didn't want to ship the dog. The woman was pregnant and the family wasn't going to have room to take the dog with them.

So I told her that I wanted to meet the dog first to make sure we were compatible. I met the dog and he was nice, so I agreed to take him. She paid me probably more than what just a regular passenger would have paid me to share expenses.

So we hit the open road. The dog barked one time during the entire drive, and that was in a hotel because he heard a train or something.

We were driving through west Texas in the middle of nowhere. We were near Fort Stockton, Texas when all of a sudden one of the tires blew out. It seemed as if I was like the only person on that road. Off in the distance, I could see that there was a structure of some kind. I looked at the tire and saw that it was in ribbons, so I couldn't hurt it any more. So I drove probably about a mile to this structure. I pulled in and saw that it was a gas station and thought I must be the luckiest guy in the world. However, no such luck. Not only was it closed, it had been abandoned. So I pulled onto the concrete and unloaded everything from the trunk because the spare tire was in there. Everything I owned was in this car. I stacked everything on the concrete next to the car.

Up a hill behind this abandoned gas station was a house with a sidewalk or steps going up. I finally got the car up on the jack and down the steps came this woman ... with a shotgun.

I said, "Hello."

She yelled, *"Get off my property!"*

I said, "Ma'am, I've got a flat tire. I'm just going to change the tire and then I'm gone."

"Get off my property!"

"Ma'am, I've got the car up on the jack ..."

"Get off it *now.*"

By now she was looking straight at me and was aiming the shotgun directly at me. She was maybe fifteen feet from me. I said something, and she fired the shotgun right over my head. I think I wet myself; I'm not sure. I started throwing stuff in my car, just cramming everything in. I was shaking so bad.

I got in the car with a flat tire banging on the ground and drove until I was out of sight of this place and sat there for I don't know how long trying to compose myself. I was still shaking so bad that I cut my sweaty hands to ribbons when I finally changed the tire. The rim had been worn down so much. It was razor thin because I drove so far on the flat.

And all the time, this dog was just sitting there looking at me. He didn't bark the whole time. I dropped off the dog in Las Vegas and then ventured back home to Los Angeles to patch things up with my mother.

Me with my cross country driving companion. This photo was taken *before* the woman fired her shotgun at me.

This section began about people I knew and had come across during my early years. But I digressed. I was talking about Faith Radenbaugh.

Faith had a friend named Evelyn Orowitz, a good-looking redhead. Evelyn was Miss New Jersey and the two of them hung out a lot during the Miss Universe contest. Evelyn's brother was the national junior javelin champion and was out in LA at the time being recruited by USC. Evelyn's brother was born with the name Eugene Orowitz, but the world would later come to know him as Hollywood actor Michael Landon.

Faith's older brother was the coach of a Little League team in the LA area and one of the kids on his team was a player named Rick Dempsey – the same guy who'd go on to star for the Baltimore Orioles in the 1970s and '80s. After Rick's playing days, he would get into coaching and managing and ironically he spent the 1997 and 1998 seasons as my manager in Norfolk.

But I digress.

My relationship with Faith ended in 1954. Right after we broke up, I was going to work a football game between LA State and UC Santa Barbara. I was scheduled to work as a member of the chain crew during the game. I drove to Santa Barbara with several of my friends for the game. One of them was dating a gal named Jackie Frankland, who also was in the car.

After the game, all of us went out and had a few drinks and somehow she ended up leaving my friend and ended up with me.

And three weeks later, we were married in Las Vegas. Yes, I got married after only knowing Jackie for three weeks.

It lasted about a year and a half or something like that. She just didn't want to be married. She had been married previously, got pregnant, got divorced; she was like 17 or something. She didn't think she could support the child and gave the baby up for adoption. She had terrible self-esteem. She felt like she had done something terrible. She was a beautiful girl, but she just didn't think much of herself. She was a bright girl and a very talented artist. She just didn't know what to do with herself. The marriage just didn't work, and that was a bit of a blow to me. I wasn't used to failing at anything. I haven't failed at a lot of stuff in my life.

I don't talk about that marriage very much because it was a very brief encounter in the overall scheme of my life. I have no idea what happened to her.

Meanwhile, I kept on doing what I was doing. I was going to school, playing baseball and trying to get my degree. And I was working. I had to work to support myself and I had some interesting jobs.

I drove a cab in Los Angeles during college. I knew LA really well from playing ball all over the place; so I knew where everything was. One night, I picked up a guy on the Sunset Strip after the bars closed at two o'clock. He got in the cab and I said, "Where can I take you sir?"

He said, "County Jail."

I said, "I don't think they have visiting hours this time of night."

He said, "No. I'm turning myself in."

I said, "Excuse me."

He said, "Just take me there."

So I did what he asked and I didn't ask any questions. I pulled up in front of County Jail. He handed me a hundred dollar bill. The cab ride was maybe five dollars. He said, "You might as well have it. They'll screw me out of it in there anyway." He got out of the cab and that's the last I ever saw of him.

While I was going to school, I had the best job I'd ever had money-wise, working for a temporary labor business called Miller Carlson in downtown Los Angeles. I was the office manager and was taking home more than $200 a week. That was a lot of money in 1955. I was going to school full-time at Cal State LA getting the GI Bill. But I wasn't happy. I hated the job because guys were down on their luck. The office was on skid row. Guys came to California to seek their fortune and didn't have enough money to wait for a paycheck, so they worked day-to-day and we weren't supposed to help them get a permanent job. If they were any good, you wanted them working for you. Miller Carlson paid people a dollar per hour. You'd write them a check for eight hours and the check was like for $7.74. They'd stay at the Prince Edward Hotel for two bucks a night. They had enough left over to maybe eat. It was just terrible.

It was a well-paying job, but I really hated it. The two guys who owned the company were based out of Chicago. One of them came to Los Angeles and had lunch with me one Friday afternoon in February 1956. He said, "You're doing a great job for me and I really appreciate it. What are your plans now that you've got a degree?"

I told him, "I don't really know what my plans are, but I've got to tell you that I hate this job. I really want to quit." The guy was surprised. I told him it was so depressing seeing some of these guys who are good people and I couldn't help them and they were trapped in this situation.

"We really don't want you to quit. Is it money?"

"No. If anything, you probably overpay me. I really just don't want to do this. As a matter of fact, I really want to quit and I'll give you notice, but I'll stay until you find somebody to take my place." That was my last day working for Miller Carlson. I got paid a month's severance and we parted ways.

That same night, I went out to dinner to celebrate and it was a tremendous load off my mind. When I was at the restaurant, I happened to run into a friend of mine. I told the guy I had just quit my job earlier that day and the guy asked me if I was interested in getting back into baseball. I told him that I didn't want to get back into the game as a player. I had hurt my arm and didn't want to play anymore. My days as a professional baseball player were done. My dream of being a major league catcher had been long forgotten.

My friend said, "I'm not talking about playing. I mean in the front office."

I said, "Yeah, I'd like that, but who in the hell would hire me? I've got no experience."

He said, "I know these guys with this minor league team in Bakersfield. They don't have a general manager for their team. You know all the scouts in southern California, Babe Herman, Danny Regan, Johnny Moore, Rosey Gilhousen and all these guys. They would recommend you. Let me give you a guy's name and you call him Monday morning."

So Monday morning, I called Sam Tobias, owner of the San Joaquin Tractor Company and also one of owners of the Bakersfield Boosters of the California League.

Sam said, "We've almost decided on somebody for the job, but when can you drive up here?"

"I can drive up today."

"We'll see you at two o'clock then."

So I jumped up and got dressed, got in the car and drove two hours to Bakersfield. I walked in and there were five guys sitting in a circle with a chair in the middle. Resumes hadn't been invented yet and they barely asked me any questions. They just asked me to tell them about myself. So I started talking. And I kept talking. And they finally asked a question or two.

"Can you keep books?" they asked. Accounting was not high on my list of skills and qualifications, but I wasn't about to let on.

"Well, of course I can."

I digress back to spring of 1948.

I was a college freshman at UCLA and I was on my second major in my second semester. I was a theater major my first semester. I was playing freshman baseball and I had this accounting class like at one o'clock, so I was never there. So one day, the professor said to me, "Stay after class Mr. Rosenfield."

"Why are you never here?" he asked. "You do fine on the tests, but you're never here."

I said, "Because I really made a mistake. I play baseball and I shouldn't have taken this class at one o'clock. I have to be at practice and games and so on."

He said, "I'm probably going to have to flunk you."

"Well, I pass all the tests."

"Yeah, but you don't do anything in class. You never add anything to the discussion." Then he said, "You play Southern Cal this weekend, right?"

"Yeah."

"If you beat Southern Cal, maybe I'll pass you."

I proceeded to get five hits but we lost 14-13. It was probably the best day I ever had. But we still got beat. So I go to school on Monday and I was real depressed. He beckoned me with his finger and called me up after class.

"Got beat, huh?" he said.

"Yes sir."

"I see in the *Daily Bruin* that you had a pretty good day."

"Yes sir, I did."

"Well, if you pass the final, I'll pass you in the class."

That was the extent of my experience in accounting.

Back to my interview in Bakersfield.

These five guys told me to go across the street to get a cup of coffee while they discuss me. I don't even think I got through my first cup when they came and got me.

"If we give you the job, when could you start?" the panel asked.

"Today?"

They said, "All right – you have the job!"

One thing I didn't know at the time was that there was a guy sitting in the outer office who thought he had the job. He was there when I arrived and he was still there when I left. So without the panel even speaking to Babe Herman, Johnny Moore and Rosey Gilhousen or anybody else, I was given the job. I was 26 years old and I was the general manager of the Bakersfield Boosters, a low-level Class C independent minor league baseball team in the California League.

My career in Minor League Baseball has begun.

CHAPTER SEVEN

BEGINNING IN BAKERSFIELD

What the heck was I going to do now? I realized several years earlier that I was not going to be a major league player, but I never thought about working in the minor leagues. I thought about becoming a radio broadcaster, but what did I know about actually running a team? I guess I had experience with some of the logistical things when I put together the team in the Navy. But this job was going to be very different. It was about running a business, and I never really thought of baseball as a business.

I got paid $450 a month and my job was primarily to run the administrative side of the organization. I knew the game of baseball but I knew nothing about selling tickets, selling advertising, selling popcorn, or even keeping books. I had to learn on the fly. Because we operated independent of a Major League club, I was also involved in acquiring players, which I enjoyed because that really put me in touch with the on-field product. We made a small profit that first year, but the team lost a lot of games. The Boosters went 48-92 and finished forty three games out of first place that season. It was my first introduction to how little wins and losses impact the financial bottom line in minor league baseball.

I was the organization's only full-time employee. I had a lady that came in and oversaw the concessions on game night. I had a guy that came in and ran the tickets. I did everything else, including the concessions reports every day. The ticket guy and the concessions person would make up the bank deposit every day and I had to balance. I did one hundred percent of the books. Good thing I passed that accounting class in college!

I was afraid to ask anybody in Bakersfield anything. Any time I had a question, I called somebody in Los Angeles because I was afraid they'd find out I didn't know anything. I learned the hard way.

I was pretty young and I had a lot of fun people who worked for me on game days. Concessions people, a couple of people who worked the gates. And we used to party pretty hard.

In those days, all of our beverages were in bottles. We had investors from Coca-Cola, Pepsi-Cola, 7-Up and Canada Dry bottlers. There was no fountain syrup. So we had to have all bottles. We had six or seven kinds of soft drinks, six or seven kinds of beer. All the drinks came in these big wet tanks, giant metal tanks in which you'd put blocks of ice. The ice would melt into water and you had to go in there and fish out a beer or soda. The only way you could really keep track of your money and your inventory was by stacking the empty cases at the back of the stand.

The next day, I would come by and check them and I'd mark them. When the concessions staff would come in, they would move them to the warehouse. I did my stand sheets based on the count of the empties. The employees finally figured out the system. They would wait until I was out in the stands and they would take a stack of maybe five beer cases – that's a hundred and twenty beers worth fifty cents each – to the warehouse and take exactly $60 out of the till. They'd take a partial stack of soda and they'd take exactly that amount of money. The next day, I'd come in and look at the stand sheets and the stand sheets would come out right on the money.

We weren't doing monthly statements. All of a sudden, we got to the end of the year and our concessions profit had gone to hell. For the life of me I couldn't figure out how it happened. I'd finally looked and knew we sold more stuff than that. I took all the invoices from all the beer and soda we had purchased against what we had sold, and there was a huge discrepancy. They probably got five or seven thousand dollars by taking $50 to $120 a day. They found a way to steal and they stole a lot of money.

As I learned the ropes, I became more and more aware of importance of the small things, and how important it was for me to know every brick, every door, every splinter of the ballpark.

I relied heavily on Marvin Milkes, the general manager of the Fresno Cardinals, to really show me the ropes of how to run a minor league team. Marvin would go on to become general manager of the Seattle Pilots in 1969.

In those days, you had to do all of the player personnel paperwork – disabled list, player transfers; you had to do everything. The first couple of years, I was the batting practice catcher and I coached third base most of the time. I was even on the active roster some of the time.

1956 was really a whirlwind of a time for me. It was my first time really away from home, other than two years in the Navy and a short stint in Daytona Beach. Bakersfield is only a couple of hours away from Los Angeles, but I was really on my own. I would come back to LA occasionally to see family or friends because I didn't really know anybody in Bakersfield yet.

The team photo from my first year in Bakersfield

My college roommate was a guy named Dick Hussman. He was a real nut. He was the only guy I ever knew who took tub baths. I'd come home and he would be in a bathtub with a quart jar of martinis and a book. He was a real character. Dick was dating and eventually married a gorgeous redhead named Gail. Gail's best friend was a girl of Hungarian descent named Mata Friedman.

In early April that year, I went down to LA because Dick and I were set to take Gail and Mata on a double date. I had never met Mata. We were supposed to go out to dinner and we were supposed to pick up the girls at seven thirty. He and I got to drinking and we didn't show up until like nine or nine thirty. I guess that relationship got off to a bit of a bad start.

Mata was an adopted only child who was sick a lot as a young girl. She was very spoiled, very bright, very quiet. She was on-guard all of the time, worried she'd be hurt by something. She read a lot. I guess I came around at the right time. Or perhaps it was the other way around.

But she got over me being late to our first date. In fact, three weeks later, we were married.

So Mata and I began our new life together in Bakersfield just after the start of my first season as general manager of the Boosters. I worked a lot and Mata was very supportive as my career was getting started. I was learning how to be a general manager, which I thought I was pretty good at. I was also learning how to be a husband. I told Mata that there were two things I could promise her. I would never lie to her and I would be faithful to her. But I had a lot to learn about being a husband. I worked an awful lot in those first few years. (I guess I worked an awful lot for the decades that would follow as well.) But at that time, I threw everything I had into my job.

Our wedding photo. From left - Dick Hussman, me, Mata, and Gail

In 1957, we changed the team's name to the Bears, and our fortunes on the field began to turn around as well. In my second season, the team's record improved to 65-74 as a Chicago Cubs affiliate. But something else happened that season that haunted me for a long time. I don't want to digress to re-live this story, but it had a major impact on me for a long time.

I was driving home one night on a residential street, going maybe twenty or twenty five miles per hour. All of a sudden, a woman jumped out from in between two parked cars to cross the street, and I hit her. And I can almost still see her on the hood of my car. The woman ended up dying and I was terrified.

The following day, the Bakersfield newspaper had a headline that read "WOMAN, 66, KILLED – BASEBALL MANAGER CITED." I got a ticket because in California, they have the basic speed law. If you're going even only one mile per hour and you hit something or someone, it's your fault. They had a coroner's inquest to see if I was going to be charged with vehicular manslaughter. Fortunately, this woman's daughter, who lived in Santa Barbara, came forward and testified that her mother had said to her two days prior to the accident, "Don't worry about making funeral arrangements for me. I've already made my own arrangements for my demise."

So it was concluded that she had done it deliberately and I was absolved. I went back to the newspaper because they hadn't yet written a story reporting that I was not liable for the woman's death. I was enough of a public figure in the community to warrant a headline, but the fact I was absolved and that story didn't even make the paper – I didn't think that was fair. People in the community were looking at me not knowing what to say, not even wanting to look at me. I just didn't think that was fair. Ultimately the paper did run a story clearing me and clearing my name.

Anyway, I did kill a woman, and the image of what happened is something that took me a long time to recover from.

Right after that season, Mata give birth to our only child, a son named Marc. Now I had to learn how to be a father on top of everything else. I was fortunate to have Mata at home raising Marc. It was interesting trying to raise Marc with Mata because our backgrounds were so different. She had rheumatic fever as a child so she was coddled and pampered. She was an only child and I was the youngest of eight children.

But I digress.

Much against my wishes, our board of directors let our manager go with fifteen days left in the 1957 season, which was pretty pointless to begin with. We were with the Cubs, but we had been trying to get another working agreement with Philadelphia and Babe Herman was scouting for the Phillies. So Babe came in as our manager.

Babe was a great player and was a hero of mine growing up. When I was a kid, he was playing for the Hollywood Stars. He was a great, great pinch hitter. To get to know him personally was a pretty big thrill for me. He was one of the most notable power hitters during his 11-year Major League career with the Brooklyn Robins/Dodgers, Reds, Cubs, Pirates and Tigers. He wouldn't ride the bus with our team. He would drive his Cadillac. He said, "I haven't ridden the bus in thirty five years and I'm not starting now." He would take a nap on the bench. He was a real character.

In December 1957, following my second season in Bakersfield, the Baseball Winter Meetings were held in Colorado Springs. My board of directors had given me something like three or four hundred dollars to get there, to stay in a hotel, to eat and whatever else. How the hell was I going to survive at this convention on only a few hundred bucks? I had gone on the train with Babe Herman and Danny Regan, who had signed me with Philadelphia seven years before. We ended up in the club car all the way from Los Angeles to Colorado Springs. Babe Herman had all the money in the world and I had none. I think Danny Regan had less than me. Babe still hasn't reached for a check. He's been dead since 1987 and he ain't reaching now!

In addition to his long career in baseball, Babe Herman was also a turkey rancher. He told Regan and me stories about how much money he'd have if he could raise the price of turkeys a quarter of a cent per pound.

Babe Herman

Upon arriving at the Winter Meetings, I met a former minor league player and minor league manager named Tommy Giordano. Giordano had come to Colorado Springs looking for a front office or scouting job in baseball. He had played for eleven seasons, including the last few as a player-manager in the Milwaukee Braves organization. Neither Tom nor I had very much money, so we ended up rooming together during the convention. Tom ended up becoming one of the most well respected scouts in professional baseball for the next five decades. We've remained close friends to this day.

We ended up getting the working agreement with Philadelphia for the 1958 season. It was really a special year for me because that's when I started working with Paul Owens. The Phillies named Paul Owens to be our field manager for the 1958 season. Owens twice hit .400 in the minor leagues in a playing career that was interrupted by World War II. He was on our roster as a player-manager, but he got very little playing time. He was absolutely great with young players. He was a father figure who really knew how to bring them along – knew when to kick them in the ass and when to pat them on the back. He was outstanding.

Paul spent two years with me as my manager. We became so close that he ended up moving to Bakersfield after the two years that he managed us. He became a scout for the Phillies and then became the farm director, general manager and was even their field manager for a short time. Everyone who knew him called him "The Pope." He was a great, great guy.

We remained friends for more than four decades until Paul passed away in 2003.

In 1958 we went 84-55 and won the California League championship. Not only was Paul Owens becoming a dear friend, he also was the field manager the final time I put on a uniform.

Both of the Bears catchers had gotten hurt. One of them was injured during a game, and the other guy fell off a motorcycle. The latter was Nolan Campbell, a local kid who was the star of the Bakersfield College team. I had helped sign him to a Bears contract and he lost his eligibility when I signed him. I almost got lynched for signing him.

Paul Owens

Owens approached me in desperate need of somebody to put on the tools of ignorance. "You catch batting practice for us. Do you think you could catch for a couple games until one of these guys comes back?"

I said, "Yeah, I probably can."

So I was in the lineup when we were on the road in Visalia playing the Cincinnati Reds affiliate. The home plate umpire was future Hall of Famer Doug Harvey, who I had played against in college when Harvey went to San Diego State. Doug and I were friends. He was a California League umpire and worked games in Bakersfield from 1958-60. He even met his future wife, Joy Glascock, when she worked for me as an usher. Doug and Joy were married in 1960 and remain married to this day.

A kid named Bob Bubash, who threw harder and was wilder than anybody on our staff, was the pitcher. He walked ten and struck out ten and probably threw five hundred pitches that game. A lot of those pitches were in the dirt, coming up and hitting me. I was getting beaten to death. Every time I get hit, Harvey was back there laughing. Somewhere along the line, nobody was on base for a change. Bubash threw another one in the dirt and I just let it go and the ball hit Harvey. Now he started cursing me. I said, "You've been laughing at me all game."

But getting hit with these balls was not the worst part. The humiliating part was there was a left-handed pitcher against us – David Skaugstad - and a left-handed hitter batting ahead of me in the lineup. There were two guys on base and Skaugstad walked the left-handed hitter to get to me. How embarrassing. But I showed him. I drew a walk to force in a run, resulting in an RBI. That was the last competitive game I ever played in and it was the final at bat of my illustrious career.

It was commonplace for Hollywood entertainers to come to Bakersfield to test their new material before they moved on to the glitz and glamour of Las Vegas. They would come for a week and get all the wrinkles out. One such performer was my old college friend, Billy Barty. He came to town to do some stand-up comedy, a little singing, a little dancing. Mata and I went to see him and had a great time. We invited Billy to our home for a Sunday afternoon dinner.

Our son Marc was two years old at the time. We kept saying to Marc, "One of dad's friends is coming to dinner. He's about your size, but he's a grown-up, so you shouldn't say anything about his size to him." So Billy pulled up in the driveway in his little car and immediately got out of the car. We had this huge boxer dog that bolted out of the house because he was so excited to see Billy. He ran to the driveway and immediately knocked Billy on his butt. Billy was filthy. We got him up and tried to clean him off and we got him into the house. Marc was waiting just inside the front door, took one look at Billy, and immediately said, "Hi. How come you're so little?"

We all laughed about it and ended up having a great time, but I should have know better than to tell a kid not to say something, because they are going to do just the opposite.

Marc and me in 1959

Bakersfield was a great experience for me starting off in the business of minor league baseball. Being a one-man operation, I learned it all and seemingly did it all -- including nearly burning down a stadium. We were getting down to the end of the season one of those years and we were in a dogfight with the Fresno club for first place. We were going back and forth with them in the standings. One of us was up by a half-game and then it would flip flop. It was a great race. The race came down to the last day of the season and Fresno was up by a half game entering play that afternoon. We had a double-header scheduled against Reno and Fresno had a double-header rained out that same day in Salinas. We had to overtake them in the standings and we definitely had to win both games.

It hardly ever rained in Bakersfield. In fact, in five years there we were only rained out twice. But it rained that day like a son of a bitch. We had to play those games because if not, we were going to lose the pennant. The place was a complete quagmire.

I knew a guy that owned a gasoline company. I got hold of him at home and said, "I need you to get me a tank truck of gasoline." I called I guy I knew a guy with the lumber mill. "I need sawdust."

I got them to bring this shit out. We covered the infield with sawdust and gasoline. We were going to burn the field. That's how you tried to dry out fields back then. Well, nobody would get near this thing except me. I lit the thing and almost burned the freakin' place down. There were flames forty feet high. It was the biggest mess you'd ever seen. I lit the fire and had to run like hell because it was following me.

Anyway we split the double-header and finished a half game behind Fresno in the standings. I was upset because I went through all of that due to the fact I wanted to win so badly. Winning was important to me. It's still important to me because I'm competitive. If you ask me, it's what our game is all about. Making money is the icing on the cake.

But I digress.

Me with sportswriter Mary Garber in 1957. The big news of the day was that the New York Giants were moving to California the next season (photo courtesy *The Bakersfield Californian*).

Our 1960 club in Bakersfield was pretty good. We scored a lot of runs and it was a pretty entertaining team to watch. One night, we were playing the Visalia club, which was managed by a guy named Bill Robertson. They were not very good that year. We were scoring a lot of runs against his team. I looked over and he got the umpire's attention and he called time out from the top step of his dugout. He motioned to the umpire that he was making a pitching change.

I saw Bill later and said to him, "Bill, I saw you make that pitching change from the dugout. I have never seen that before. What happened?"

Bill said to me, "Dave, I was so tired of going to the mound and having guys talk me out of taking them out of the game. I just didn't want to be talked out of it again. If I don't go out there, they can't talk me out of it." It was one of the funniest things I ever saw on a baseball field.

A few years later, once we had moved to Portsmouth, I was sitting in my office and in walked the same Bill Robertson. He lived in Suffolk and we became very good friends. We socialized for a number of years together. He had gotten out of baseball and became a peanut buyer.

Anyway, my fifth season in Bakersfield had just ended. My board of directors was chirping at me about a few things. I felt I'd been there long enough that I ought to move up or do something, and so in September, I'd really made up my mind I was going to leave. I told them I was going to go ahead and resign. I told the board, "I'm tired about arguing over little things that we shouldn't be arguing about and you probably don't need a general manager now until January. You can save three or four month's salary. So let's part as friends."

They said, "Okay."

I came home and told Mata, "Sit down. Let's have a drink." We made a drink and I said again, "You need to sit down."

Mata said, "Why do I need to sit down?"

"Well, because I think you do."

So she sat down and said, "Alright, what happened?"

"I just quit."

I didn't know what I was going to do. I only knew I wanted to stay in baseball.

I knew a guy who owned an imported car dealership in Bakersfield. The man called me when he read in the newspaper that I had resigned my position with the Bears. "What are you going to do?" he asked.

I said, "Well, I'm going to stay in baseball, but I'm not going to do anything until the first of the year."

"Well, why don't you come work for me and sell cars?"

"I don't want to be a car salesman."

The guy said, "Well you need to do something. Don't you need the money?"

"Yeah. I do need the money." I told the guy that I couldn't be a typical car salesman and BS people about how good a used car is. I said, "I just won't do that."

"You're a good salesman. I don't expect you to lie to anyone. Do whatever you want."

So I accepted the job and worked for the dealership for three months, working four hours per day. I'd come home and it was like I'd worked 18 hours. It was awful. I remember Mata saying to me, "You better go get a job in baseball because if not, you and I aren't going to be around anymore because you are not the same person now as you were. You are not happy."

And she was right. So I went to the 1960 Baseball Winter Meetings in Louisville and got a baseball job in Topeka for the 1961 season.

CHAPTER EIGHT

SOMEWHERE OVER THE RAINBOW

I was now the general manager of the Topeka Reds in the Class B Illinois-Indiana-Iowa League, better known as the Three-I League. The Three-I League had been a force in Minor League Baseball for the first 60 years of the century. It was the nation's oldest Class B minor league, then the highest level of low minor leagues.

The year in Topeka was slightly unbelievable from the time I took the job. In fact, I was never told that the team owed nearly everyone in the Western hemisphere. I was trying to operate a ballclub with no money and a constant lien against the bank account by the IRS, the State of Kansas and plenty of other creditors who stood at the end of a very long line. On top of that, the Three-I League would end up folding after that season.

The weather in Kansas was the absolute worst that I ever saw. The winter was a never-ending blizzard, the summer was about two degrees hotter than the fires of Hell, the wind never got below about 20 MPH and there was a tornado every other day. Mata and Marc spent the summer in the bathtub, as the recommended safe spot in a house with no basement. The theory was that the tub was anchored to the foundation and wouldn't head for Oz when the storms hit.

The saving grace of that year was that the club was outstanding and won the pennant under the guidance of Player-Manager Dave Bristol, who went on to manage several Major League clubs. Prominent players on the Reds included Tommy Harper, Tommy Helms, Art Shamsky, Teddy Davidson, Vic Davalillo and several Cuban players.

The Cuban kids made up a big part of Cincinnati's minor league system because a man named Bobby Maduro had owned the Havana Sugar Kings of the International League and signed a lot of players for the Reds. When Fidel Castro took over in 1960 the Havana club moved to Jersey City and Cincinnati held on to the players.

On Opening Day we had the players lined up on the foul lines for introductions and all the usual hoopla, and as we started to play the Star Spangled Banner, outfielder Marty Dihigo, whose father, a great player referred to as the Cuban Babe Ruth, turned his back on the flag and faced the grandstand. I knew that Dave Bristol, who taught U.S. History in the off season, would probably kill Dihigo if I didn't intervene. I hurried to the clubhouse as the players went in to prepare for the game and several guys were holding Bristol back as he tried to get at Dihigo. Bristol was yelling "I'm going to kill you or if I can't, I'm going to send you back to Cuba on a *bus.*" It wasn't very funny at that moment, but when you think about it calmly, his line was hilarious.

The league had Des Moines, Cedar Rapids and Burlington in Iowa, Lincoln, Nebraska and Fox Cites (Appleton) in Wisconsin, where Earl Weaver was the skipper. It was a close race between Earl and Bristol to see who was thrown out of the most games. Bristol won by a nose!!!

The club had a great (in comparison to the past) year at the gate and actually made money. This was the only time in my fifty-plus years in the game that I had a written agreement about pay and bonuses, and it is the only time that I ever failed to receive what I was due. That season was a great learning experience for me, and I guess it helped to prepare me for all things that lay ahead.

We were at the Winter Meetings having emergency meeting after emergency meeting to try to save the league. Most of the working agreements had moved to the Carolina League. We were meeting morning, afternoon and night. Farm directors tried to help us. We all wanted to save the Three-I League.

The president of the National Association (governing body of Minor League Baseball) was George Trautman, an old baseball guy for a thousand years. He had a nose that looked like a potato. He drank like a fish. And I wound up sitting next to him at all of these meetings. He had breath like the fart of a dragon. He would turn and talk to me and it would just about knock me out of my chair. Anyway, when I left the Winter Meetings, I thought we'd saved the league.

With Mata and Marc in tow, we drove to California for Christmas. When we arrived at my mother's house, mom said I had a message from George Trautman. I called – the league had folded. So now I was sitting in Los Angeles with a house full of furniture in Topeka, without a job and the Winter Meetings are over.

The job I really wanted was Santa Barbara in the California League, but I didn't get it. Al Gionfriddo, the old outfielder with the Dodgers and Pirates, had retired as a player and became the general manager in Santa Barbara. That was the job I really wanted because it was a great town and my mother wasn't doing particularly well.

My job search resulted in two offers. One offer was for a very interesting job in Waterloo, Iowa, in the Midwest League. The job would have me running the ball club and also running an arena that was next to the ballpark. I didn't know anything about that. It probably would have been a pretty good career thing to learn how to do that.

The other offer was as the assistant general manager of the Tidewater Tides in the Class-A South Atlantic League. Millionaire sportsman Bill McDonald, who promoted the 1964 Cassius Clay-Sonny Liston heavyweight championship fight, owned the Tides. He also owned the Atlanta Crackers in the International League and the Tampa Tarpons in the Florida State League. The Tides general manager was Marshall Fox, a veteran baseball guy who had been in Tampa for years. He was hated by a lot of people. When Pat Corrales played for him, Pat and a couple other guys went up to the office and fired guns through the door and everything else. They really hated the guy. I don't think they even knew if he was in there.

Joe Ryan, who later became the president of the American Association, oversaw all three of McDonald's clubs. I knew Joe Ryan, but I didn't know him real, real well. Joe told me, "Marshall Fox has had a heart attack. He's going to have the title of general manager and you're going to have the title of assistant general manager, but you're going to have to run the club. Marshall probably won't even be at the ballpark half the time." Fox had in fact had a heart attack, but was also a hypochondriac.

I said, "Joe, I don't want to be an assistant. I've already been a general manager for six years."

Joe said, "I need somebody there who can run the club. If you do this, I will take good care of you."

Weighing the two offers, I didn't know what I wanted to do, but I knew I didn't want to be an assistant. Christmas was over. We loaded up the car and drove back to Topeka from LA. We got there and there was like 18,000 feet of snow. We couldn't get in the driveway and had to park in the middle of our front lawn. Marc was four years old. We packed up the house, called a moving company and asked them to pick up our stuff on Tuesday.

They asked, "Where are we taking it?"

I said, "I don't know. I'll call you on Monday and tell you if it's going to Iowa or Virginia."

We took off and drove to Waterloo. I wanted to see the place. I hadn't accepted either job nor had I turned down anything. I had either job. We stayed in Waterloo for two days. The high temperature in those two days was six-below. Mata and I talked and talked the whole two days we were there. From a personal standpoint, there was no question that I wanted to get the hell out of that weather. But it was a good job. It was probably going to pay a little more and the idea of learning how to run an arena was kind of enticing. But I had spent one dreadful year in Topeka in terrible weather. You'd freeze your ass off in the winter and die in the summertime. Mata was a California kid and there was no damn way I could live in that again. It was worse than Topeka. So I declined. It was so damn cold. Unbelievable.

While still in Waterloo, I made two telephone calls -- one to Joe Ryan and one to the moving company. I was headed to Portsmouth, Virginia to be assistant general manager of the Tidewater Tides.

1961 Topeka Reds Baseball Club

Back Row (l to r) Gen. Mgr. Dave Rosenfield, Dick Hopkins, Sam Thompson, Marty Dihigo, Art Shamsky, Harvey Alex, John Flavin, Mel Queen, Stan Jones, Pres. Sherman Huff

Middle Row (l to r) Al Kinney, Miles McWilliams, Marty Zambrano, Mickey Mattiace, Mgr. Dave Bristol, Gerry Dawson, Bill Reeves, Ted Davidson, Larry Rancourt

Front Row (l to r) Batboy Doug Wright, Al Suarez, Ivan Davis, Tommy Harper, Tommy Helms, Batboy Buddy McCune.

CHAPTER NINE

VIRGINIA IS FOR BASEBALL LOVERS

My first season in Portsmouth was a really difficult year. I'd known Marshall Fox. He and I got along okay. Joe Ryan was right – half the time, Marshall was nowhere near the park. He'd call me at five o'clock in the afternoon to ask me if the flags were up. I'd say, "Marshall, I've operated a ball club for six years. I know how to run a ballpark!"

Fox had a big black reclining chair in his usually vacant office. The chair came in handy when I had to put drops in Marshall's eyes to remedy a medical problem he had with his eyes. Occasionally, Mata would put the drops in his eyes if she was around the office.

We only had one other full-time employee besides me, a woman named Valerie Marshall. She was our bookkeeper/ secretary/office manager/whatever the hell else. She was a character. She stayed with me until the mid '70s.

About mid-way through the season, Joe Ryan came to town. I had already had about enough being the assistant to an absentee boss. I said, "Joe, I've got to tell you right now, in order to be perfectly fair to you, I'm not going to do this again next year."

Ryan replied, "Don't worry about it. I'm going to take care of you. My present thought is that I'm going to move Marshall back to Tampa and you'll have this club."

I decided to trust Joe Ryan and said okay.

After the season ended, Marshall Fox and I drove to Charlotte for a South Atlantic League meeting. Joe Ryan met us there. The three of us had breakfast before the meeting started. We talked about this, that and the other. There was no comment from Ryan about anything we'd discussed regarding moving Marshall to Tampa or anything.

We got to the league meeting and the president of the league, Sam Smith, called the meeting to order. He asked for any initial comments before getting into the agenda. Joe Ryan held up his hand and said, "Mr. President, we return the Tidewater franchise to the South Atlantic League." In those days, franchises had no monetary value whatsoever. He literally gave the franchise away.

Shock set over the room, especially over Marshall and me. Essentially, Joe Ryan not only just fired us but he also killed a franchise. We weren't able to address this with Joe until after the meeting. Marshall was almost whimpering to Ryan. "What's going to happen? What are you going to do?"

Ryan responded, "Marshall, I'm going to move you back to Tampa. Don't worry about it."

I said something and Joe Ryan said, "Dave, don't worry about it. I'll take care of you. We'll work something out."

More than fifty years have passed since that conversation. I've yet to get another check from Joe Ryan.

I didn't know what to do. I was 3,000 miles away from where I'd want to be out of work if I was going to be out of work. But I thought Portsmouth was still a pretty good place for a ball club and even though we had only been there less than a year, I liked the community and felt baseball could be successful there.

The first football game I went to in the area was on a gorgeous fall day in the fall of 1962. William & Mary vs. Virginia Military Institute. I went with a guy named Herb Simpson, who was the director of civil defense for the city of Portsmouth. I had been talking to Herb about saving baseball and organizing a franchise. Herb said there was going to be a guy at the game who would be very helpful to us in our endeavors. Herb wanted me to meet this guy, Dick Davis. Dick, a graduate of the College of William & Mary, was there by himself. He was watching the game with a briefcase full of scotch, having a drink and just having a nice afternoon. Herb introduced us and I had all of my financial projections on sheets from a yellow pad in my pocket. Dick looked at me like I was a bastard at a family reunion. I took my two or three sheets and handed them to him and he all but threw them on the ground. He really kind of dismissed us and I was kind of taken aback by that.

About a week later, I went to talk Bill Lewis, a Chevy dealer and an important guy in Portsmouth. Bill said that we really needed a lawyer to put the thing together and to help us form a corporation. He said, "I've got the perfect guy. Be in my office at two o'clock and I'll introduce you to the guy I really want to be involved in this."

Dick Davis

I walked in to his office that afternoon, and there stood the guy Bill Lewis wanted me to meet – Dick Davis. I thought to myself, "Here's the end of this deal. Just a week ago, I had tried pretty hard to interest him and he wasn't buying in to it."

I guess Dick's friendship with Bill Lewis convinced him that he should be part of it after all.

We had kind of a mass meeting of people that we thought would be interested and we were looking for people to say they'd invest $200 or $500. Nobody was doing anything. We didn't have one person step up with even a dollar. Dick Davis finally turned to Bill Lewis and said, "You got a counter check? Give me one of your checks."

Bill Lewis reached in to his briefcase, pulled out a check, and crossed out the name on the check. Dick wrote a check for $500 and then everybody started putting money in. We raised $9600 during that meeting, a lot of it in ten dollar shares. If it weren't for Dick Davis, I wouldn't be here today and baseball might not be here today. I get more credit now for saving baseball in this area, and that probably isn't fair. Yes, I pushed hard, but I did not have the credibility in this community. I had only been there for 11 or 12 months. They didn't know me from Adam's off ox. His credibility in the community led these other guys to say, "Alright, we're in."

Dick Wood, who was head of the Portsmouth Chamber of Commerce, was disturbed about losing the team. He thought maybe we could somehow get into the Carolina League, which geographically was really better for us. Dick got a few people together to talk about it in the early fall of 1962.

Subsequently, I contacted the Carolina League president Bill Jessup. Jessup was a perfect old southern gentleman with a mane of white hair. He was a very dignified man who always wore a nice suit. He was also the Budweiser distributor in Wilson, North Carolina. Jessup told me that the Carolina League would be very interested in adding the Portsmouth club into their league, but only if they could get another franchise to join at the same time. The league was not about to have an odd-number of teams because of difficulties with scheduling, travel and several other reasons. The other stipulation Jessup included was this second team would have to be geographically close to Norfolk.

Professional baseball had a rich history in the Tidewater area, serving as home to minor league teams continuously for decades. Norfolk had teams dating back to 1894 with the Clam Eaters, followed by the Jewels (1898), Skippers (1901), Tars (1906-18 and 1922-55), Mary Janes (1919-20) and All-Stars (1921). The first team to be called the "Tides" was the '61 South Atlantic League team. Portsmouth had the Browns (1901), the Truckers (1906-10 and on-and-off from 1914-35), the Pirates (1912-13), the Cubs (1936-52) and the Merrimacs (1953-55). Newport News had the Shipbuilders (on-and-off from 1901-22), the Pilots (1942) and the Baby Dodgers (1944-55).

I reached out to some business people on the peninsula (Newport News, Hampton and the surrounding communities) for help. There was a guy who had come here as general manager of the Baby Dodgers named Vic Zodda. Baseball left this area in 1955 because the old Piedmont League folded. Vic stayed in Newport News, got into the restaurant business and made a fortune in restaurant and hotel management. He ran 25 or 50 hotels and a couple of very nice restaurants on the peninsula. He was very interested in bringing baseball back to the peninsula. He got some people together. The one caveat to getting them involved was that they had to have a working agreement with a Major League team. Independent teams did exist, but they weren't as successful on or off the field as teams that had direct affiliations with Major League clubs.

Needing to find a working agreement with a Major League club, I starting calling around to see what I could do to save professional baseball in the area. I knew Walter Brock, then the farm director of the Washington Senators. Brock was with the Kansas City Athletics when I was in Topeka in 1961. Walter said the Senators wanted to have a team in the Carolina League if we could get a franchise approved. He said, "If you can get in, you've got yourself a working agreement."

The problem was getting the second working agreement to satisfy Bill Jessup's stipulation for getting into the Carolina League. Nobody in the Portsmouth or Norfolk areas wanted to front any money to me for a franchise until they knew they'd get a team. The Portsmouth Chamber agreed to pay for my trip to the 1962 Winter Meetings in Rochester with the agreement that, if we got into the Carolina League, the new team would reimburse the Chamber for whatever I spent. So I went to Rochester. Walter Brock and I tried every which way to find another working agreement, but we couldn't find one anywhere. We left the Winter Meetings without a working agreement.

I came back to Portsmouth and hatched up an idea. I knew enough people in the game. I knew I could get ballplayers. I had a lot of teams tell me they'd give me one player here, two players there, or someone would give me three. I knew we could operate this thing independently. So I approached Vic Zodda and told him I couldn't get a second working agreement. But if he would give me $5000 for the working agreement I had with the Washington Senators, my club would operate as an independent and we'd both get into the Carolina League. Zodda agreed, professional baseball was saved in the area, and the Tides were now part of the Carolina League. I think it's the only time anybody's ever heard of somebody selling a working agreement.

I had nothing in writing, but I obviously told Walter Brock, and he was agreeable. Brock told me he'd prefer to be working with me rather than someone else, but he was just happy to be in the Carolina League. The Hampton ballpark was decent, but the Portsmouth ballpark was better.

Tidewater Community Baseball, the group we put together to move the club into the Carolina League, started the 1963 season with $9600 in stock. Dick Davis, Bill Lewis, Dick Wood, Ed Garland and Herb Bangel were the ones primarily involved in getting this group off the ground.

As a new member of the Carolina League, I attended the league's scheduling meeting in January 1963. Bill Jessup handed out a schedule for us to look at. In those days, there were 20 weeks in a schedule. I thought I was going to look at a schedule that had us playing roughly 20 Fridays and Saturdays at home. I looked at this thing – we had seven Fridays and Saturdays. *Seven!* The guy who had made the schedule was from Winston-Salem, and they had like 30

Fridays and Saturdays. I was pretty disturbed. Jessup asked the room if anybody had any comments. I held up my hand.

Jessup said to me, "*New boy*, what have you got to say?"

I said, "Mr. President, aren't weekends supposed to be equally distributed among all the teams?"

Jessup replied, "What do you mean?"

"We ought to be entitled to around 20 Fridays and Saturdays. We have seven. I note that Winston-Salem has like 30. That isn't fair."

Jessup said, "You think you can do better?"

I made one of the greatest statements of my life. I said, "*A monkey could do better!*"

Jessup said, "You've got two weeks to present a better schedule."

I had never thought about how to make a schedule. So I came back home and started to fool around with it and I made a schedule. And it was adopted almost unanimously. The only team that didn't approve it was Winston-Salem. And I've been making schedules ever since.

Schedule making has been kind of a passion of mine. I've made schedules for many leagues since and I've been the only schedule-maker the International League has known since 1969. It takes me about two hundred hours to make a schedule, depending on how big the league is. It's a terribly tedious job and I usually do it all by hand. There were no computers back when I started making schedules. I'd write them out on napkins and legal pads. The thing is, it's so important that schedules be fair. At our level, the difference between having a Friday or Saturday versus a Monday through Thursday is probably at least $25,000. It's not right that somebody have three or four less than their fair share. You can't do that to people. The other thing is the travel has to be equitable. Why should somebody have to make 10 trips and someone else make only six? I've just always thought it was so important that it be fair.

The one bad thing about making schedules is that your club can't get any advantage. I do not submit schedules where anyone has less than 21 Fridays and Saturdays in our 22-week schedule. Now, I get criticized that teams have too many weekend dates in April and May. I can't make everyone happy all the time.

But I digress. Not only did I feel I had to fight for a fair and amenable schedule, I felt it was more important for me to be a civil rights crusader as well.

Racially, the south was very tough in the early 1960s. It was still segregated. Black players weren't allowed to eat in white restaurants and they had to wait on the bus for their teammates to bring food to them. Black players were still prohibited from staying at the same hotel as the rest of the team. They had to stay at dumpy little places all over the place while their white teammates would stay at places that were usually nicer and in better areas. We had four or five black players at the time. It was really bad for them and I had had enough.

Our team usually stayed at a place in Winston-Salem called the Zinzendorf Hotel. I called the hotel and said, "If you don't take our whole team, we aren't coming there." I had no idea where the team was going to stay, but it didn't matter to me. I needed to take a stand for our team and for the black players. I was insistent, and the hotel knew it. After putting up a fight, the Zinzendorf finally agreed to let our entire team stay there.

So I was feeling pretty good. I thought I was the champion for the black players on our team. I called them into my office and told them, "For the first time, you're staying with the team."

They looked at me and said, "Really? We're going to be able to stay with the whole team?"

"Yep, absolutely."

So shortly after that, the team went on the road to Winston-Salem. It was early in the season. The team came back from the road trip. One of the black players, Alvin Cooper, came to my office and knocked on my door. "Dave, can we talk to you?" He led two or three of his black teammates into my office to meet with me.

Alvin said, "We really appreciate what you've done. Nobody has ever stood up for us like that before. It really means a lot to us. But the Zinzendorf is one *terrible* hotel. Please don't make us stay there again. Can we stay at the other one from now on?"

The Zinzendorf Hotel in Winston, NC

I said, "Your ass is staying at the Zinzendorf and you can suffer like the rest of the team!"

But I digress. Back to 1963 to our first season in the Carolina League ...

Portsmouth Stadium was allegedly the first cantilever ballpark in the country. It had a tremendous amount of foul territory because longtime owner Frank D. Lawrence loved watching catchers go after foul balls. It was really a nice ballpark.

Frank once sued Major League Baseball -- took it all the way to the Supreme Court – over invasion of his territory by television. It was a landmark case. He hired James P. McGranery, the former U.S. Attorney General, as his lawyer.

Frank D. Lawrence Stadium in Portsmouth

One of the justices of the Supreme Court had his eyes closed during the proceedings. Mr. Lawrence went up to him and pounded on the bench and said, "Wake up! This is important!" Not surprisingly, he lost the case.

Mr. Lawrence owned and operated teams in Portsmouth for nearly a half century before baseball folded in 1955. He was a lovely, lovely man. He was president emeritus of

American National Bank when I came to town and really took a liking to me.

He decided he was going to have a Hall of Fame at Portsmouth Stadium. He had a guy take 4x8 sheets of plywood and frame them and hang them on the concrete walls enclosing the concourse. That's where his Hall of Fame was going to be. He inducted practically everybody he'd ever met. He'd gotten to know me and I'd told him my mother had been an actress and all that and he said, "I'm going to put your mother in the Hall of Fame."

I said, "Mr. Lawrence, you haven't even met her."

Lawrence said, "But she had you and that's good enough for me."

So Estelle Rosenfield/Therese Lyon went into the Frank D. Lawrence Hall of Fame at Portsmouth Stadium. Mr. Lawrence was such a kind man that once, during a business trip to San Francisco, he made a detour to Los Angeles with the express purpose of meeting my mother for the first time. That's what kind of guy he was.

Frank D. Lawrence

We renamed the ballpark "Frank D. Lawrence Stadium" in 1964 in his honor, two years before he passed away. The park remained standing until the city tore it down in 1997.

Portsmouth Stadium was not in a great neighborhood. There was a lot of poverty around the area and we had break-ins all the time. We used to have to have a watchman stationed overnight just to keep an eye on the facility. We had this room off the concourse that was the night watchman's room. It was hot as hell in there. He had a lawn chair in there that he used to sleep on and he drank like hell. He'd lay on this chair and go to sleep. We were playing on the peninsula one night and got back to Portsmouth at one o'clock in the morning after a game. He's laying on this freakin' chair sound asleep. Players picked him up, in the chair and took him out to center field and set him out there. We had the sprinklers on a timer and he wakes up in the middle of the night with the sprinklers soaking him.

But I digress. I was describing the bad neighborhood that surrounded the stadium.

It was not uncommon to hear the sound of police sirens serenading the air in the few blocks surrounding the old park. One time, I heard these sirens and I came out and looked across to this parking lot. Across the street was a Sears store. A kid had broken in to the Sears store and he came running out with two small portable televisions and the cops running behind him. This kid got to the stadium gates, which were closed. He dropped the televisions, got through the gates, up this little hill and went across the field. The two cops who were chasing him just stopped and were looking at me. What could we do? We just laughed.

This area was pretty bad. Mata even got mugged on the concourse during a game. Somebody came up behind her and stole her purse and almost jerked her arm off.

Ed Nottle was a longtime minor league pitcher who won eleven games for the Tides in 1965. He had been a paratrooper and he came up with an idea that season. He said to me, "One of these games that I'm going to start, why don't I jump out of a plane, land on the mound and start pitching?"

I thought pretty seriously about it and said, "The problem is, if you miss by about one block, you're going to end up in somebody's yard and this is a pretty rough neighborhood. I think we better skip that idea."

But I digress.

The Tidewater Tides operated as an independent club in 1963 and I was responsible for everything from player acquisition to the operation of the business end of the organization. We had our own Spring Training and had to run everything independent of any Major League backing. I hired Al Jones to be our field manager. Jones had been a Triple-A catcher in San Diego, Toronto and Jacksonville and was previously a coach in Jacksonville. I knew Jones from the Navy, when Jones played at the San Diego Naval Station. As a matter of fact, he joined our team when we were playing for the Service Championship of the World. We were allowed to pick up guys from our district during the tournament. Anyway, after we picked him up, I almost never caught again. I was the back-up catcher to start with and once Al came in, our regular guy became the back-up because Al was pretty darn good.

Anyway, Al and I ran a tryout camp, signed some local players and started begging and borrowing from here, there and everywhere to put their roster together. We played local colleges and a couple of service teams for Spring Training games. A couple of guys came to us on loan from Major League teams who paid part of the salaries. Detroit sent me a couple of guys. The Phillies sent me guys. Paul Owens was close to me and I'd worked with the Phillies in Bakersfield. They tried to help me.

Hank Peters, longtime baseball executive and one-time Kansas City farm director, once asked me during the Winter Meetings about Porterville, California because Peters was considering taking the A's there for Spring Training. I said, "Why don't you think about training in my ballpark in Bakersfield? I can probably get the county to let you use the ballpark for very little. I can help you with anything you need."

Paul Owens with Mata and me

Peters said, "You'd do that?"

I said I would, and we made a deal to bring them to Bakersfield and Peters trained for two years at Sam Lynn Park. He kind of owed me one. Peters was still with Kansas City in 1963 and he sent some players to the Tides, including big Larry Stahl who went on to play for the Kansas City

Athletics and New York Mets. We were kind of the last place for guys who had been in their organizations for a while. Maybe they were troublemakers or maybe none of the managers really wanted them. If for whatever reason the organizations didn't want to release them, they sent these guys to me. It was really a strange kind of team.

We'd gotten a guy who had been a big prospect for the White Sox, but they didn't know what the hell to do with him. He was this big left-handed pitcher who had a terrible win-loss record for us. He was just awful and his failures on the field really were eating at him. Jones called me in the middle of the night once when the team was on the road. Al said, "Shit! I was just up on the roof of the hotel."

I said, "What were you doing up there?"

Jones said, "I had to keep this guy from jumping."

Somewhat sarcastically, I said, *"Why'd you stop him?"*

In the middle of the season, somebody called me and said that Detroit had just released probably the best pitcher in the Florida State League, a left-handed pitcher named Lindy Kurt. This guy was a bit of a character, giving fans the finger, grabbing his crotch to the umpire, all kinds of stuff. Detroit finally had enough and released him. But this guy told me Kurt could pitch, so I signed him. He ended up pitching a no hitter for us.

On paper at the end of the year, we lost about $3500. The board of directors kept calling me throughout the season asking if I needed more money. I kept telling them no and that I could get by. Operating as an independent club for the first time and losing only $3500 was pretty respectable.

The Tides went 65-79 that strange independent year – ultimately finishing ahead of the Peninsula club that had the full working agreement with the Washington Senators, a team which featured a 19-year old outfielder named Lou Piniella.

We went to the Winter Meetings in San Diego and Dick Davis and I were sitting in the back of the room at the draft and all of a sudden, I heard, "The Los Angeles Dodgers select from the Tidewater club, the contract of left-handed pitcher Lindon Kurt."

The Dodgers had to pay us four grand for his contract. I stood up and yelled, *"We broke even!"*

A full working agreement finally came to Tidewater in 1964 when we hooked up with the Chicago White Sox. The first four players in that squad's lineup combined to steal more than 200 bases. We had nearly twice as many stolen bases (219) as any other club in the Carolina League. Ed Stroud (72), Buddy Bradford (50), Joe Jones (50) and Cotton Clayton (30) set the base paths ablaze that season. If they got on base, they ran. It was a fun team to watch. In that ballpark with all that foul territory, if a pitcher threw the ball away trying to pick a runner off first, we were liable to score.

We ended up with a very respectable 75-63 record and finished second in our division.

I remember a really fun evening that happened during that 1964 season ...

During that year, we hosted two Major League exhibition games. The New York Mets played the Baltimore Orioles on Friday and the Washington Senators and Pittsburgh Pirates played the Saturday afternoon. As travel arrangements would have it, all four teams would be staying overnight on Friday, allowing us to host a casual dinner for approximately 70 people – the local press, the club directors and the managers and coaches of the Major League teams. It was held in a private room with a bar set up for the guests.

I was host and emcee of this evening. I informed the managers of the teams that this was going to be a strictly informal dinner. I told them I wanted them to take about two minutes each and come to the front of the room and say, "We're glad to be here." They could say something about their team if they wanted to. If not, just thank everyone for coming. It was very casual, no need to take up any time at all.

The first three managers obliged and did exactly what I requested. Pittsburgh's Danny Murtaugh spoke first and was followed in order by the Orioles' Hank Bauer and Washington's Gil Hodges. The fourth speaker in the lineup was the Mets' skipper, the legendary Casey Stengel. Stengel was two years away from being voted into the Baseball Hall of Fame.

Stengel and Dick Davis, our president, were talking about banking throughout this whole dinner. They were alternating going to the bar and getting each other glasses of scotch. They were having a hell of a time. I saved Stengel to be the last speaker. So I finally introduced him and he got up and spoke. I reminded him that he only needed to speak for a couple of minutes. He spoke for an hour! He had people on the floor – he was absolutely hilarious. All of the things you've read about him talking – he was all of it. When he finally finished talking, he turned to me and said, "*Boy*, you told me I didn't have to talk for more than two minutes. What the hell did you tell me that for?" That was an unbelievable evening – the people who were there will never forget that one.

But I digress. I was talking about our on-field performance.

We were good and exciting in 1964, but the 1965 team was able to win the Carolina League championship. We had four pitchers win at least 10 games and that club stole 169 bases that season. That season ended up being our final as a White Sox affiliate, thanks to some brilliant decision-making by me.

The Carolina League, a few years removed from resisting an odd number of teams in their circuit, now in fact, did have eleven teams in 1966. I think it might have been the only eleven-team league that's ever been. We played mixed double-headers where you'd play two different teams on the same day. You'd have two days off in a row every twenty days. By 1966, Paul Owens had become the farm director of the Phillies. Paul and I really wanted our teams to work together since we had known each other for so long and we were such good friends. I convinced our board of directors to make the switch. We told the White Sox, who had just won us the league championship, to leave and we went with the Phillies. We promptly finished in eleventh place in an 11-team league. Larry Bonko, the caustic and sarcastic writer who covered us for the afternoon newspaper, *The Ledger-Star*, wrote an article about that team that started: "What has 18 legs and lives in the cellar? The answer is the Tidewater Tides." It was a great line, even though I wasn't laughing at the time. Our record that season was 58-81.

Off the field, things weren't much better. I'll never forget this story that happened during that season. The name has been omitted to protect the guilty.

There was a kid who grew up in Portsmouth and hung around the ballpark. He was a nice kid, loved baseball. He used to hang numbers on the manual scoreboard. He used to run errands and one thing or another. And he ultimately became my trainer. Trainers didn't have to be certified back then. Scotch tape, band aids, ice. That's all they needed.

Anyway, one of my dear friends was a guy named Rick Current, who was the general manager of the Carolina

League team in Rocky Mount where our team was playing one night. He called me at like two o'clock in the morning.

Rick said, "I hate to have to call you with this, but they have just arrested your trainer."

I said, "For what?"

Rick said, "I really don't know. They're saying it's a crime against nature."

I said, "What in the hell does that mean? Was he trying to hump a tree? What does that mean?"

"I don't have any idea, but you better get down here."

So I said, "Okay."

So I got dressed and jumped in the car and headed south for the 120 mile drive to Rocky Mount, North Carolina. Former great Negro League player Buck Leonard happened to be the probation officer. My guy had been arrested on charges of trying to solicit sexual favors. Rick and I got them to drop the charges and it was a very quiet two-hour drive back home.

The 1966 season wasn't all bad and full of hilarious after-the-fact drama. In fact, Paul Owens reached out to me before the season to ask for a favor. He said, "We've got a very wealthy young guy who wants to get involved in baseball and potentially buy a club. He's talked to (Phillies General Manager) John Quinn and we're thinking about having him go and spend most of the season with Eddie Leishman (general manager of the in Phillies Triple-A club in San Diego). But I think it would be better if he came and spent time with you. If he goes to San Diego, everything is more departmentalized, and he really wants to learn about how a team works. If he comes to you, he'll see every bit of it – he'll see concessions, ad sales, he'll see everything because you do it all. Would you be agreeable to him spending time with you?"

At my desk in 1966 or 1967

I said I'd like to meet the guy and if we seemed to get along, he could come spend time with me. The guy came in and I agreed to let him hang out and observe how I did things and how a team was run. He was a very nice guy. He'd fly in on Monday morning and every place I went, he'd go with me. Ad sales, anything I did, he'd stay right with me. He'd go home on the weekend if we didn't have anything going on and he'd come back the next Monday. And then during the season, he'd come in for homestands.

About a third of the way into the season, I suggested to the kid that he should see some other kinds of operations. I told him that I was kind of a middle of the road promoter and operator. I told him he needed to see somebody who did nothing as far as promotions and that he had to see somebody who was kind of promotion-happy. I told him, "You need to determine for yourself what you think. I want you to do that and then you come back and we'll talk about what you see and what you like and so on."

I sent him to Macon, Georgia, which was where the Phillies Double-A club was located. The general manager was a guy named Art Kowalski who did nothing but open the door. No promotions or anything. Then I sent him to spend ten days with Pat Williams and the Spartanburg Phillies (Philadelphia's Single-A affiliate in the Western Carolina League).

Pat Williams, who would go on to a legendary career in the NBA as an executive with the Chicago Bulls, Atlanta Hawks, Philadelphia 76ers and Orlando Magic, was known to be a protégé of master promoter Bill Veeck. When Veeck owned the St. Louis Browns, he became famous for bringing in three foot seven inch Eddie Gaedel to pinch-hit during a regular season game. Pat Williams used to do all kinds of Veeck stuff – two gorillas wrestling and all kinds of stuff.

The kid spent about a week and a half with Pat. When he arrived back in Portsmouth, we reviewed and discussed his observations, what he liked and so forth. I ultimately advised him not to purchase a club for a while. I told him that I thought he should take a job in the game first to see if he really liked doing it seven days a week. I said, "You've seen it on your own terms four or five days a week. That's not the way it is. I can help you get a job. You don't need the money. Somebody'd be thrilled to death to have you. See how you really like it."

Within about two weeks, the guy had purchased the York White Roses in the Eastern League. He got totally hoodwinked and found out the club owed umpty-umpt thousands of dollars that he had to pay off. He ended up buying the Tucson club later and was later the president of the Pacific Coast League and the International League. Toledo's General Manager, Charlie Senger, used to call this guy "The Phantom" because he could never find him. As radio host Paul Harvey would say, and that guy was Roy Jackson ... owner of 2006 Kentucky Derby winner Barbaro. He was a great guy. Philadelphia Main Line. Loads of money. His dad died and left him about eight zillion dollars. His mother re-married somebody with even more money. I've always thought that someday he'd own a Major League team, but he never has."

Because of the continual interaction between us as we were running our respective clubs, Pat Williams and I became good friends.

I was a conservative type of club operator who believed fans came to games simply because they wanted to see baseball. Pat would say I ran our club with no frills. No dog and pony shows. Pat was completely opposite in his philosophy. The differences in our philosophies never created a wedge in our relationship. He is now a celebrated author and motivational speaker who tours the country giving infectious speeches on leadership, teamwork and relationships.

Pat loved to talk on the phone late at night. He'd call me at eleven or midnight, even later sometimes just to talk. He had left Spartanburg to go to the Sixers and then he went to Chicago to become GM of the Bulls. He called me one night at some ungodly hour after his first year with the Bulls. I asked him, "Well, how'd you do this season?"

Pat said, "We doubled our revenue."

I said, "That isn't what I asked you. I asked how you did."

Pat said, "Well, we doubled our expenses."

So I said, "Then you lost twice as much money as your predecessor."

Pat joked, "I'm not calling you anymore."

But Pat does call me still. When he comes to town, he'll call and we'll get together for dinner or just talk. A couple of years ago, we went to dinner at the Inn at Regent University in Virginia Beach. I was eating a steak and starting choking on a piece of meat. Pat jumped up and performed the Heimlich maneuver on me. The meat flew out of my mouth, as did my false teeth. It was quite a scene. *What a sight!* I grabbed my teeth and put them back in. We barely missed a beat, sat back down and went on with the conversation. Pat said we were going to have hamburger from now on. No more steaks.

Pat's son Bobby was the Washington Nationals farm director from 2007-2009 and I said I would help him any way I could. He called me asking about possibly getting an affiliation with Syracuse and I put him in contact with Tex Simone and John Simone, owners of the Syracuse club.

I never did take on all the Veeck-type stuff that Pat did, but gradually I came to realize that the game itself wasn't enough anymore. If you wanted to bring in families, it got to a point that you needed to do more entertaining in addition to the game.

One of the most well known entertainers in our business was a guy named Max Patkin. Max was known as "The Clown Prince of Baseball." He was a barnstorming performer and played minor league stadiums throughout North America from 1944-1993. He had a face seemingly made of rubber that could make a thousand shapes. He wore a uniform with a question mark on the back rather than a number. He was beloved all across the country and really became popular again after he appeared in the 1988 movie *Bull Durham*.

I booked him my first year and brought him back every year. I probably booked him more than anyone else in our business. When Max was getting close to the end of his career, I asked him for a favor.

Max said, "What's that?"

"I want your last show." Max agreed.

I told him, "But I know you're gonna screw me. You're gonna commit for the show and then you'll go and do something like die and I won't get your last show." And that's exactly what happened. I didn't get his last show.

One night after a show in Portsmouth, Max came with Dick Davis and me and several other people to a private place called the Midtown Club and we had a few beverages. Max got running his mouth as he often did and started talking, not worrying about offending anyone. No subject was off-limits.

Max said, "Anybody who smoked a pipe is probably gay."

Dick Davis was a constant pipe smoker. Dick very calmly reached into his pocket and took out his pipe. He got out his tobacco. He was sitting where Max was not looking directly at him. He lit his pipe and tapped me on the shoulder.

Dick says loud enough for everyone to hear, "Do we have to book him anymore?" Patkin turned and looked at Dick. Max and everyone immediately burst out laughing. To the last time I ever saw Max, we'd still laugh about that.

**Another favorite photo of mine showing Max Patkin and
me having some fun during a rain delay sometime in the 1980s**

Hall of Fame pitcher Bob Feller was another guy who used to tour around minor league ballparks. He'd throw batting practice to sponsors and media, he'd speak to Rotary Clubs and sign autographs for fans. As one of the greatest pitchers in baseball history, Feller was revered across the country. I would schedule Feller to come in to town so that he could speak at a dinner at a local sports club one night and then appear at the Tides game the next night, thereby sharing the appearance fee. At one of these particular dinner appearances in the later 1970s, Feller stepped up to the microphone and proceeded to tell the audience everything that was wrong about baseball. I don't know when I was ever so upset.

I approached Feller after the dinner was over. I said, "Bob, you've just done your last show for me."

He said, "What are you talking about?"

I said, "I've spent my life trying to convince everybody in this community that baseball is a great thing and how it's a great way to spend an evening. It's a wholesome outing for the family. And you proceed to go out and tell people what a terrible thing it is. 'The ownership is wrong, the players are terrible.' You've done your last show for me. Here's your money. I don't even want you on the field tomorrow." I cancelled the show, gave him his appearance fee and sent him on his way.

At the following year's Winter Meetings, Feller approached me. He said, "I want to thank you. Everything that I am and have in this world, I owe to baseball. You really woke me up. I will never do that again."

But I digress. We're still in the mid-1960s and things were going pretty well for us overall.

The legendary Buck O'Neil was one of the many iconic baseball people I've been fortunate to know in my career

Professional football had come to the Tidewater area. The Continental Football League, born in 1965 and led by former baseball commissioner Happy Chandler, was intended to be a competitor to the National Football League.

The Continental League wanted to be completely independent from the NFL - they didn't want players, money, or any other means of help from the NFL. A local group owned and operated a franchise called the Norfolk Neptunes from 1965-1967, but they struggled financially for all three seasons. The local group that owned the Neptunes went through more than $200,000 they had raised to operate the club and then went through an additional $150,000. The Neptunes were in trouble.

Dick Davis was a marvelous man. Every time something would happen in the community he thought we ought to get involved in, he'd call me and say, "I want to meet you for breakfast." When he made those calls, I knew something was coming up. Dick wanted to rescue the sinking Neptune ship. "The football team's in trouble," Dick said. "We can't let them fold. We gotta get involved." So we sold about $100,000 more stocks, changed the company name to Tidewater Professional Sports and took over the football team.

In addition to running the Tides, I also ran the Neptunes for three seasons – 1968, 1969 and 1970. We really did a good job turning things around. The franchise averaged in excess of 13,000 fans per game and we were widely considered the most successful franchise in the league.

I didn't agree with the mentality that the Continental League should be completely independent from the NFL. I felt that the Neptunes should get help from wherever they could find help.

In their infinite wisdom, the Continental League did not want to be a feeder league. They wanted to compete with the NFL, which I thought was pretty stupid.

George Hughes, who was a two-time All-Pro guard during a five-year career with the Pittsburgh Steelers, was one of the Neptunes' head coaches while I was general manager. He was a wonderful, wonderful, wonderful guy. He was a local guy who went to high school here. He went to college at William & Mary and was an All-American there. He fought in World War II and was a gunner on a Flying Fortress. He was a school board member and was ultimately a city council member in Norfolk.

Art Rooney, the legendary owner of the Steelers, had a fond relationship with Hughes dating back to when Hughes played for the Steelers in the 1950s. Hughes called Mr. Rooney to see if we could visit him to talk about some help for the Neptunes.

Legendary Steelers owner Art Rooney

George and I flew to Pittsburgh and we were ushered in to see Mr. Rooney. He was hugging George and kissing him, throwing his arms around him. We sat there for like two or two and a half hours talking and Mr. Rooney didn't want to talk about football. He wanted to talk about baseball. He was a huge baseball fan. I had read someplace that he never missed a Pirates game. He wanted to talk about the Tides, everything about our team. We kept trying to switch it to football, but he wanted to talk about baseball.

Around eleven thirty or noon, Mr. Rooney said that he was going to take us to lunch at his club, which was in walking distance. Mr. Rooney walked out from around his desk and said that we had to make a stop at the shoemaker along the way. Mr. Rooney was in his socks. He had dropped off his shoes to be half-soled. So the three of us were walking down the street in Pittsburgh with Mr. Rooney, the icon of all icons in Pittsburgh, walking along in his socks. I wish I had a camera. Ultimately, Mr. Rooney sent us three or four players, paid all their salaries and was very helpful to us.

The Neptunes' partners in the league weren't as fortunate relative to off the field success. The problem was the league had so many weak franchises that would fold and just not show up. After two years, we joined up with another league called the Atlantic Coast League. That league ceased operations after the 1970 season without ever making a formal announcement of their demise.

But I digress.

CHAPTER TEN

MEET THE METS

Major League Baseball added two teams in 1961 (Los Angeles Angels and Washington Senators) and again in 1962 (New York Mets and Houston Colt .45s), bringing the total number of clubs to 22. The next round of expansion was on the horizon for the 1969 season, as four more teams would be joining the big leagues (Kansas City Royals, Seattle Pilots, Montreal Expos and San Diego Padres).

Major League Baseball coming to a city that was already home to a minor league club meant the minor league franchise had to find somewhere else to play. The Phillies' Triple-A club in San Diego was in that very situation – which meant the Phillies were going to need a new city for their Triple-A team in three years.

In 1966, Paul Owens had talked to me about the possibility of Philadelphia moving their Triple-A affiliation to Tidewater when MLB expansion would force San Diego's Pacific Coast League franchise to move. By 1968, I really wanted to elevate Tidewater to the Triple-A International League (IL). John Quinn (who was the Phillies General Manager at the time) and Pat Williams (from the Phillies affiliate in Spartanburg) were both on the expansion and realignment committee. I felt like we had a couple of people on our side if it got to that. But there were no franchises available in the International League. Nobody wanted to sell a franchise or give it up at that point. The Phillies couldn't wait anymore, so they moved from San Diego to Eugene, Oregon with their Triple-A club.

We had made a pretty persuasive argument that Tidewater would be a pretty good Triple-A territory. We had done some artist's renderings of what we could do with Lawrence Stadium to accommodate Triple-A baseball. Attention switched to trouble spots in the make-up of the International League and particular focus went on the Jacksonville Suns franchise. The IL was not thrilled with Jacksonville being in the league geographically and the Mets, who owned the club, were losing their hat and ass down there. The IL was pretty well paired up geographically (Buffalo and Toledo, Rochester and Syracuse, Charleston and Columbus), meaning teams could easily bus between the two cities on road trips. The expansion and realignment committee felt that Tidewater would make a good situation in the IL because it would be a better geographical partner with Richmond than Jacksonville was. They kind of persuaded the Mets to look at coming here.

Mets representatives came and spoke to the city of Norfolk about building a ballpark and participating in some fashion. They really liked the idea of coming to the Tidewater area, but they didn't like the idea of upgrading Lawrence Stadium. There was much greater population on the east side of the Elizabeth River and the Mets wanted to see what could be done about building a new park.

The discussions gained momentum and the Mets gained more and more confidence that the Norfolk area would be a great situation for them. The Mets agreed to pay for half the stadium. The issue that remained outstanding was who was going to own the new Triple-A club. The Tides owned the territory, but the Mets owned the Jacksonville club that they wanted to relocate to Norfolk. The Mets wanted sole ownership, but we wanted to enter into a joint venture in which the Mets agreed to pay the Tides at least $25,000 from profit.

Johnny Murphy, a former longtime Yankees relief pitcher, was the Mets' General Manager. Murphy told me that the Mets wanted me to remain on as the Tides General Manager. I told Murphy, "John, I won't do that. If you come in on an ownership, I will not accept that job. I don't think it will be successful. This is still the South. We want to get our community behind this operation. If we do well and send a bunch of money to a millionaire in New York (referring to Mrs. Joan Payson, the Mets' owner) – that will not be well received."

Murphy said, "You serious?"

I said, "As serious as can be."

Murphy said, "Okay."

Murphy, Mrs. Payson and the Mets' directors now had to debate whether to work with our current group or come in on an ownership basis. Dick Davis and I flew to New York to meet with the entire Mets Board of Directors. We first met in the Park Avenue apartment of M. Donald Grant, the Mets chairman of the board. The meeting then moved to a boardroom in Shea Stadium.

Donald Grant was chairman of the stock brokerage firm Fahnstock & Company – and he was Mrs. Payson's stockbroker. A group of wealthy people were sitting around on a yacht one night. They were all talking about what they would like to do, their secret ambitions. Donald Grant said, "I would like to sit in the owner's box of a Major League Baseball team and be in charge of the company."

So, many years later when the Mets were created and Mrs. Payson became the owner, she called Donald Grant and said, "I remember once sitting on my yacht that you said you wanted to be in charge of a Major League Baseball team. Would you still like that?" And he said yes, so be became chairman of the board.

From left to right -- George Weiss, Casey Stengel and Hank Bauer

Anyway, we went into this boardroom and all their directors took their seats around this table. Future Hall of Famer George Weiss, who had kind of been a hero of mine as a Major League operator, and Johnny Murphy, Mrs. Payson, Dick Davis – a pretty exemplary group of people.

There was not a seat at the table for me. There was a couch on the side, and I was sitting on the arm of the couch like a complete idiot. Dick Davis, a great Southern gentleman, white hair, extremely articulate, got up because they asked him why we thought it ought to be a joint venture of some sort rather than them operating the team. Dick stood up and gave this very flowery, persuasive speech. He finished and they were all kind of nodding their heads.

Johnny Murphy stood up and said, "Regardless of what the decision is here today, I've asked Mr. Rosenfield to be our general manager in Tidewater."

I stood up from my perch sitting on the arm of the couch and said, "Mr. Murphy, please tell these folks that I've already told you that unless the local group is involved, I have declined your kind offer to be the general manager." These people's heads all turned around like they were on swivels, looking at me.

Somebody asked, "Mr. Rosenfield, why is that?"

I said, "I do not think it will be a successful operation strictly with a New York base."

Dick and I were both excused from the room so the board could discuss what had just transpired. We were called back into the room less than five minutes later.

The board said, "We have decided based on what you've said that the best way to operate this team is as how you've suggested – as a joint venture." The Mets and Tides were now officially tied.

As the meeting started to break up, George Weiss came over to me and put his arm around me. And he said, "Son, I don't know much about you. I know you've worked in the minor leagues for a long time and now you have the chance to be a Triple-A general manager. And you have the guts to stand up for a principle you believe in. Mr. Rosenfield, you have gained my respect."

I thought that was pretty neat. It's still one of the highlights of my life.

Triple-A Baseball and the New York Mets were on their collective way to a marriage with the Tidewater Tides. The Mets essentially handed the franchise to the Tides to operate. At any time they wanted, they could take the franchise back, move it, sell it, or do whatever they wanted with it. If we had not made $25,000 as our share of the profit, the Mets would pay us that amount. So we (Tidewater Professional Sports) operated the franchise basically as a joint venture, but we operated it as if we owned it. They got a percentage of the money and we got a percentage of the net. We played that first season (1969) in Frank Lawrence Stadium while we were building Metropolitan Memorial Park (Met Park) in Norfolk.

Over the years that followed when we were in this partnership with the Mets, we only had one losing season financially – 1974. That year, we finished twenty five games under .500 and had fourteen games rained out and we lost a total of just $1,500. I'm probably as proud of that fact as anything else in my career.

The relationship with the Mets was special and pretty unique. They looked at us as if we were really the owners of the franchise. They respected me and they respected the way that I ran the club. They asked for my input in a variety of issues and I felt like they really viewed us as being part of their family. They'd often ask for my thoughts about potential managers and players.

When we first began with the Mets in 1969, a familiar face would become my first Triple-A skipper ...

When I was a kid, I kept newspaper clippings about all kinds of guys who were playing in the Major Leagues during the '30s and '40s. One of the players who happened to be the subject of one of the articles was a catcher with the Chicago Cubs named Clyde McCullough. Well, the Mets hired McCullough to be our first manager when we were elevated to Triple-A in 1969. Clyde was a complete character. He had a way of taking things and making them real. I showed him that clipping after he started managing for us, and he loved it. In fact, after I showed him that the article, Clyde used to tell people, "I've known Dave since he was ten years old."

He was a tough old guy. McCullough used to catch in the big leagues without a chest protector because it was too hot. When he was with the Cubs, the Cubs players and Chicago Bears players used to hang out at the same bar. They'd always talk about which sport was tougher. The baseball players would always say, "You've got to play every day, you've got to play hurt." The Bears players would say, "Football is so tough. You get beat up all the time."

Well, Clyde got tired of it. He said, 'You guy think you're so freakin' tough? Who's your toughest guy?"

Clyde McCullough

The Bears proudly presented Bulldog Turner, who was a six-time all-Pro NFL center in the 1940s and a linebacker who intercepted four passes in five NFL title games. Turner was one of the best two-way players in his era. Clyde said, "Run him out here." Clyde took him outside and just beat the hell out of him.

Clyde and I became very good friends. He lived in Virginia Beach for years. One night he was in a bar in Norfolk, and some guy was in there just ripping me. So Clyde just got up and punched him. He knocked him on his ass. What a character.

When Clyde was our manager in 1969, Whitey Herzog was the farm director. We didn't know each other at all. We'd talk a bit on the telephone during that first year. Whitey would ask me about the team and I told him I thought it was the strangest team in the world. We never left any runners on base. We'd run until either we scored or until we were out. Everybody ran all the time. It wasn't good. I told Whitey that.

Herzog jumped all over me for my assessment of his team. He made me feel like I was two years old. Whitey said, "What the hell do you know? Clyde McCullough's been in this game for a hundred years, and you're telling me you know more than he does?" He put me down so badly, you couldn't even believe it. I felt like I was two inches tall.

About two weeks later, Herzog came to town to see our club. He and I were sitting in the stands watching the game. At this point, I wasn't saying anything about anything. I had been put in my place properly. We got a guy on base, and he was promptly thrown out stealing. The next guy got on, and he was promptly thrown out stealing. The third guy got on, but tried to stretch a double into a triple and got thrown out at third. It was one thing after another. It was like fate had destined Whitey to see everything that I had told him about.

Whitey finally turned to me in about the seventh inning and said, "This is the god damnest thing I've ever seen! Boy, were you right!"

We went down to the clubhouse after the game and Whitey said to McCullough, "Mac, I've never seen base running quite like that. Were gonna start playing with softball rules. *No stealing!*"

That 1969 season was an unbelievable year. It was our first year in Triple-A, we were still running the football team, and we were also building the new ballpark in Norfolk. I lived in Chesapeake.

Whitey Herzog

In the morning I would start out and go to the ballpark in Portsmouth, see what was going on. I would then go to the building site of the new ballpark. I would then go to the Neptunes football office in downtown Norfolk and do whatever I had to do, usually go back to the building site again, and then if there wasn't a baseball game, I'd go to football practice. I would leave home at maybe eight o'clock in the morning and would get home at midnight or thereabouts.

Met Park was built and was the first minor league stadium that had a restaurant. M. Donald Grant of the Mets felt it was very important to have a restaurant in a ballpark. I fought the design of that ballpark. I disagreed with it completely because the restaurant was right behind home plate. We had no stands behind home plate other than four rows of 120 box seats for a few season ticket holders and players' families and scouts. The press box was at a very, very low level and the restaurant was above it. Because of the way the water table is, you couldn't have anything under ground. The clubhouses were below the press box in this building behind home plate. The players went to the clubhouses through a gate directly behind home plate.

A view of Met Park from center field shows the Diamond Club restaurant directly behind home plate

We once played an exhibition game with the Mets and Willie Mays was a coach for them at the time. He played in the game and led off, hit a home run, ran around the bases, crossed home plate and ran straight through the gate to the clubhouse, and that was the last we saw of Willie Mays.

But I digress.

I didn't have a big baseball staff to rely on to run things. I had maybe two people who worked full time for me at the Tides. I had Valerie Marshall who was our secretary/bookkeeper/whatever. And I had a young man named Alan Huggins, who was a nice kid, a character, and he did a little bit of public relations, a little bit of selling. I did almost all of the selling. There were part-time people doing concessions, including a young man who was playing basketball at Old Dominion. Pat Williams used to ask me about basketball players I'd seen, and I kept telling him about this guy. I kept telling him how good this guy was, but Pat never believed me. But he found out. This guy was Dave Twardzik, who went on to be a starting guard for the Portland Trailblazers NBA championship team in 1977.

That incredible season was the only time I ever missed a game for a reason other than illness. We had a league meeting in Columbus and something happened to my flight and I didn't get back in time for my game. The funny part of it was, Alan Huggins used to put his keys down some place, any place, and I used to tell him that you've got to put your keys in the same place all the time. Pick a pocket and that's where you always have to put your keys. If not, you're gonna lose them. You're gonna lock yourself out of some place, something's gonna happen. I keep my keys in my right hand pocket always. Never in a jacket pocket, because you might take your jacket off, but you're not normally going to take your pants off.

So sure enough, I didn't get back and Huggy left his keys on his desk and locked himself out of the office. Valerie Marshall didn't stay for games. I called Huggy from the Pittsburgh airport around five thirty to see how things were going. Of course I couldn't reach him. I got a hold of Valerie at home and she told me Huggy was going crazy because the tickets, the cash bags, everything was locked in the office. I think they ended up having to blow a door down to get everything done.

Anyway, that was a crazy year and it was the only time I missed a game when I wasn't sick.

We moved in to the new ballpark in 1970 with Chuck Hiller as our manager and it was really a different way of operating now that we had a new stadium. Everything from attendance to revenues and everything else was just elevated. The Mets had just won the World Series the year before and it was pretty neat to have all that excitement carry over to us the following year. The fans and media were all pretty thrilled with how this whole thing was working out.

The Mets were going to send Hank Bauer to us to be our manager for the 1971 season. Bauer was a three-time All-Star with the Yankees during his twelve years playing in New York from 1948-59. He also played for the Kansas City Athletics in 1960-61. He managed in the big leagues with Kansas City in 1961-62 and in Baltimore from 1964-68. His Orioles team won the World Series in 1966, sweeping the Dodgers in four games. His final year managing in the big leagues was with the Oakland Athletics in 1969. This guy had all the credentials.

We always used to bring in our manager during the off-season and have a "Meet the Manager" thing with our Season Ticket Holders. I didn't know Hank Bauer. I had met him when he was in Kansas City and I was in Topeka. And he had come through Portsmouth in 1964 for those exhibition games when Casey Stengel stole the show. But I didn't know him. All I knew about him was that he partied hard. He drank hard. I thought to myself, "I like talking to the manager after the game, having a drink or two and so on. I can't let this guy think that I cannot handle it." So he was going to be here for three or four days for this introduction. I told Mata, "This may kill me, but I'm going to hang with him. Whatever he wants to do, I'm doing it."

Well, we went someplace to dinner, had some kind of a function, and he was staying at the old Admiralty Hotel where all the visiting teams stayed. They had this after hours bar there where you had to be a member. They wanted to close, but we wouldn't let them. Hank was funny because he didn't like to drink in public. He had the tough guy image and people would come up and almost challenge him or argue with him, and he didn't want to get into it with people. What he liked to do was go to a real quiet place or to his hotel room and just sit and talk and drink. He didn't need a lot of people around. Anyway, we were in this bar at the Admiralty Hotel until 3:00, 4:00, 5:00 in the morning. Unbelievable. Finally on the third night, he said to me, "Can I please go to bed? You're about to kill me!"

I was so proud of myself. I thought I was going to die. I thought, "I stayed up with *Hank Bauer!*"

Hank Bauer

Bauer was a great guy. The two years he managed the Tides were the only seasons he ever managed in the minor leagues. His first year managing for us, he did not know how to use his whole roster. He tried to play his best guys all the time. When he needed to play his extra guys, they weren't ready to play. Having managed in the big leagues for a long time, when he needed somebody, all he had to do was bring up someone from Triple-A. Here, he didn't have that luxury.

The two seasons were pretty interesting because of the relationship between Bauer and Herzog. They would get into some pretty good arguments. I remember one that happened at my house having drinks and dinner. I thought they were going to get into a fist fight at my dinner table.

John Milner, a big and powerful left-handed hitter, was our first baseman. Milner ended up with a 12-year playing career in the major leagues with the Mets, Pirates and Expos. Milner was the first guy to wear a helmet in the field because he knew how bad his own defense was. Whitey and Hank got to talking about different guys on the ballclub.

Whitey said to Bauer, "God dammit Henry. You don't like John Milner."

Bauer replied, "What the heck do you mean I don't like him? Hell, I'm playing him every frickin' day and the guy can't even catch the ball!"

They were up on their seats in the dining room. I thought they were going to attack each other. Thank god they didn't. But that's the kind of relationship I liked having with the manager and our farm director.

When the 1970s era came to minor league baseball, uppers were huge. Everyone was taking greenies all over the place. The New York Mets became sudden death relative to drug use. One strike and you were done. The Mets told both Hank Bauer and me that if anybody got caught with amphetamines, they'd be fired on the spot. They didn't care who it was – manager, coach, player, even the trainer -- they'd be fired immediately.

Hank used to come in to the park real early. We had put a sauna in the clubhouse and he'd sit in there and sweat out the scotch from the night before. This one day, he needed an aspirin or something. So we went into the training room and went into the medical trunk. Right on the top was a frickin' bottle of greenies. I said, "What are we going to do?"

Hank said, "I know how close you are to the trainer, but your job and my job are on the line. As much as we hate to, we're going to have to fire him. He's been warned."

So we called the trainer in and fired him. The players were livid. They threatened to go on strike. They were going to revolt. Whitey Herzog happened to be in town. We told him that the players were going to refuse to play unless the trainer was reinstated. Whitey had a clubhouse meeting. Hank and I just stood there.

Whitey said, "Guys, I know how you feel, but it ain't gonna work. You want to go on strike? Be my guest. We'll forfeit tonight and tomorrow the whole Memphis team (the Mets' Double-A affiliate in the Texas League) will be here. And they will become the Tidewater Tides. You've got ten minutes to give me a decision."

We walked out of the clubhouse and went up to my office. One of the players came up and said, "We're going to play."

But I digress.

In the early 1970s, baseball was going pretty good in the area. The new stadium was great, the team was winning. We went to the playoffs in our first five seasons as a Triple-A club and won the International League championship twice in our first seven years. By now our venture into professional football had ended. But Dick Davis still had his antenna up when it came to trying to save distressed franchises or professional sports teams that were about to leave the area.

One such team was the Virginia Squires of the American Basketball Association. The team moved to Norfolk in 1970 and was owned by a guy named Earl Foreman. The Squires featured the legendary Julius Erving in 1971 and 1972. George Gervin was a Squire in 1973 but became property of the San Antonio Spurs following the season.

Mr. Foreman owed everybody in the world money and the ABA was trying to get him out of the league. There was a local group that was trying to buy the team and the league took it over pending new ownership. I ran the Squires for like two months during the 1974-75 season. They found local ownership and it looked like I was going to be the new permanent GM of the Squires.

Part of the contingency of this local group taking over the Squires was that San Antonio was going to have to sell George Gervin back to Virginia. Gerald Friedman, who was in a group that was trying to take over the franchise, joined Dick Davis and me at an ABA meeting in Chicago. We were sitting in a hotel room waiting to be called into the meeting. We had a check to give to San Antonio to get Gervin back.

And we were sitting there having coffee and Gerald Friedman says to Dick, "Richard, I have something to tell you."

Dick said, "What?"

He said, "That check you've got? It's no good. There's no money in the bank."

Dick about had a fit. He said, "Well I'm not about to hand them a check that I know is no good."

We were called into the meeting with full expectation that Gervin's contract would be sold back to us. Dick did not want to have it appear that he knew anything having to do with a bad check or with Friedman wanting to put one past the ABA or the owners of the Spurs. Dick talked around the subject during the meeting, never letting on that the check was no good.

Mike Storen, longtime basketball executive, was commissioner of the ABA. "There's a question I have to ask you Mr. Davis," Storen said. "I have heard rumors that the group you're representing may have some ties to the mafia."

Dick was looking at Storen like he had two heads. "One, Mr. Storen, it does not. But two, with the financial structure of your league, it might serve your league well if some of your franchises did, in fact, have connections to the mafia because your league wouldn't be going broke if that was the case!"

Ultimately, a different local group was successful in taking over the Squires and I wanted to continue running the team. Al Bianchi, who was the coach, and I had gotten along very well the couple of months I was involved. Al came to me and said, "Dave, I've got to tell you something. I'm going to recommend to the new owners that you *not* be the general manager."

I said, "Really?"

Bianchi said, "Yeah, unless you want to give up baseball. I know you did football and baseball at the same time. But this is too big of a job to try to do both at the same time. So unless you tell me you're going to give up baseball, I'm going to recommend they not hire you."

What he said made a lot of sense to me. So the new ownership of the Squires brought in Jack Ankerson to be their general manager. Ankerson had been with the San Antonio Spurs and the Kentucky Colonels prior to coming to the Squires. The Squires were hurting from day one because they made a strategic mistake. The league was going to charge like two million dollars or something for the franchise and you could pay it by giving it all in cash up front or by paying $50,000 a year for 40 years or some kind of payment plan. The Squires opted to pay it off immediately, and they were short of money from the beginning.

Shortly thereafter, in 1975, I experienced another one of Dick Davis' early morning telephone calls. The Detroit Red Wings had operated an American Hockey League team in Norfolk but pulled their team out of the market. Dick said, "Hockey's a good sport, we can't let that go away. We have to get involved."

My business card when I was with the Sharks

So we got involved and started a hockey team, the Tidewater Sharks of the Southern Hockey League. I ran the team for a year and then we sold it. We had a great logo. A guy who painted my fence signs at the baseball stadium designed a logo for me. It was a blue shark with pink skates.

While Ankerson was fighting to keep the basketball team afloat, I was in the same building trying to keep the hockey team going. We used to laugh about who was going to go broke first. We became very close friends and I ultimately hired him to be the Tides' Director of Broadcasting and Sales.

I had Christmas dinner at his house for like six straight years. That's what kind of friends we were. Everybody liked Jack. He was a great ambassador. We ultimately helped him become general manager of the local soccer and hockey franchises. He does the public address announcing at Harbor Park and I still have a regular weekly lunch with him and some other guys.

But I digress.

Jack Ankerson and me

One of the funniest nights of my life occurred in 1975. An old friend of mine from baseball, Rick Current, was now working for us with the Sharks and there was a hockey game on this particular night. There was this room in the arena where our booster club would have beer and the players would come in and talk to them after games. Jack, Rick and I went into the room and stayed in there until the beer was all gone and then we went into my office and drank whatever beer I had in the fridge. We went to Jack's office and drank whatever beer he had in there. Our wives had all gone home. It was probably two or three o'clock in the morning at this point. We were all feeling no pain, having a good time. I said, "There's one thing I've always wanted to do. I'd really like to drive the Zamboni."

So we went down to the ice and tried unsuccessfully to start the Zamboni. The building was dark and we couldn't get the damn thing started. So we decided to do the next best thing. Rick or Jack said, 'Why don't we go shoot a few goals?" We went and turned on all the lights in the frickin' building and the clean-up crew was all sleeping in the stands. We got a goal out and the three of us drunks were standing at the blue line shooting hockey pucks, falling down, laughing our asses off. We woke up all the cleaners who were sleeping. It was a marvelous night, a night I'll never quite forget. I'm still not sure how any of us ever got home. And I still have never driven a Zamboni.

I've always thought it's important for teams in the same city to have a good relationship and share things with each other. We're all in the same business and I don't think we should look at each other as competition.

Blake Cullen wanted to bring hockey back to Norfolk in the late 1980s. He wanted to bring a team called the Admirals into the East Coast Hockey League. I knew Blake from his days when he was the public relations man for the Chicago Cubs. He was a good man, and I told him I wanted to help him rather than look at him as being someone we're fighting for sponsors and season ticket holders. I think having another sport in the wintertime is good. And I did something for him that I don't think anybody has ever done. I sent a letter to our season ticket holders and all of our advertisers encouraging them to support Blake Cullen and the Norfolk Admirals. Blake and I are good friends to this day.

Blake Cullen

And even though baseball has been my life, it's been fun to get involved in other sports and to be able to do some different things along the way.

Anyway, back to baseball and the winning ways of the Tidewater Tides ...

In 1975, the Tides and Rochester Red Wings tied for the International League pennant, forcing a one-game playoff between the two teams to determine who would be the top seeded team in the post-season playoffs. I had a meeting with the president of the Rochester club towards the end of the regular season to determine where the tie-breaking game would be played in the event the regular season finished and the two teams were tied. We were going to have a coin flip to decide the location.

The Rochester guy said, "We'll draw a lot more people than you will, so we'll pick up some more of the expenses and why don't you let us have the game at our place?"

I said, "Not on your life."

The guy said, "Well, no one will know."

I said, "I will."

So we ended up proceeding with the coin flip and the Tides won the toss. The game would be held at Met Park. Rochester took a charter plane to Norfolk for the one-game showdown. They made their own charter reservations with Allegheny Airlines and the airline must have thought the Red Wings were a Little League team or something. They put comic books and little bags of candy on every seat of the airplane. The Rochester team was convinced I had something to do with it.

Our starting pitcher Nino Espinosa threw a strike with the first pitch and our fans began screaming and they kept screaming for nine innings. Nino, who died two years later of a heart attack, pitched a four-hit shutout and we won the game 8-0.

We ended up winning our second International League championship in four seasons. We went on to play Evansville in the 1975 Junior World Series, which pitted the champions of the International League and the American Association. We lost the series against Detroit's Triple-A club, four games to one, with the lone victory coming against Evansville's Mark Fidrych. Our manager Joe Frazier went on to manage the New York Mets the following season. Fidrych, of course, went on to become "The Bird" and was the talk of the country for all of his antics on the mound.

CHAPTER ELEVEN

ON THE RADIO

You know, speaking of broadcasting, that's really where my heart's original desire was if I couldn't play in the major leagues. I always wanted to be a radio broadcaster. When I started, not very many teams were broadcasting their games. But in Bakersfield, all of our games were on the radio. Our radio broadcaster also did Bakersfield College football and basketball. I used to do color commentary on his broadcasts during the off-season. We had the National Amateur Athletic Union track meet twice when I was there and we broadcast that nationally and also back to Australia.

But my job running a club prohibited me from being the team's radio broadcaster. But I always knew the importance of the team's broadcasts and I would be a regular in the radio booth during games. I knew that the broadcaster played such an important role in selling our product to the public. We ended up sending a number of guys to some big-time jobs after calling Tides games. I always had a passion for and a keen interest in our radio broadcasters. A guy has to have a distinctive voice and he must know the game.

When we joined the International League and became a Triple-A club, I made a radio deal with a station that we both had approval over the broadcaster. I had a bunch of resumes and tapes, and had narrowed it down to four guys that I thought would be good, and I told the station to choose the person because whoever it was would be doing a lot of selling.

Among the resumes that landed in my rejection pile during that search was a tape from Dave Van Horne, a 2011 inductee into the Baseball Hall of Fame. Van Horne spent in excess of 30 years broadcasting for the Expos and Marlins. Dom Valentino is another guy we didn't pick. He ended up broadcasting for many teams across many sports: New York Yankees, Pittsburgh Pirates, Oakland A's, New York Islanders, New York Nets, Kansas City-Omaha Kings, Cincinnati Royals and the New England Patriots.

The broadcaster we hired was a guy named Bud Kaatz. Kaatz had been broadcasting in Jacksonville for the Mets' Triple-A team where the club was prior to moving to Tidewater. He was the character of all characters.

Due to the expense involved with sending a broadcaster on the road, teams often would re-create games for their listening audience and we were no exception. The broadcaster would be in a studio getting wire feeds of what was happening in the game. With a variety of props at his disposal, the broadcaster would re-create the action by hitting two sticks together to make the sound of the ball hitting the bat. He would cup his hands over his mouth away from the microphone to mimic the sound of the crowd.

Bud hated re-creating games. He always wanted the games to be broadcast live. Bud would get so carried away. He'd start to re-create an inning and suddenly there would be a man on third and the hitter would ground out to end the inning. But in reality, the shortstop had bobbled the ball and the runner had scored. So now, the next inning if we got a run, he'd have to figure out how to take it away to get the score right. When I'd listen to broadcasts of the road games, I never gave up hope when he said we had lost the game, because I thought maybe we really hadn't.

After he worked for the Tides, Kaatz went to work at the local NBC station in Norfolk. The Virginia Squires were being coached by Al Bianchi at the time. Bud was the most annoying guy in the world and Al couldn't stand him.

Kaatz left town and serpentined across the country in a variety of broadcasting roles. After leaving the Squires in 1976, Bianchi joined the NBA's Phoenix Suns as an assistant coach. During Bianchi's introductory press conference in Phoenix, he looked up and the first person he saw was Bud Kaatz. It was like this guy was trailing him.

What a character he was. He ended up living almost across the street from me. He had two sons who got into more mischief than you can imagine. They broke my air conditioner by putting a stick in it. They did all kinds of things.

After Bud left the Tides, I hired a young broadcaster from Portsmouth by the name of Marty Brennaman. I knew Brennaman's father, who worked at Pine Grove Dairy. I knew of Marty, he had gone to college, and had been broadcasting here and there. I thought that he was an outstanding broadcaster.

Marty Brennaman

Marty and I had a great relationship and I'd go on the air with him quite often. I used to crack him up on air. Sometimes he'd come in late to do the pre-game show and didn't have time to write down the lineups. He'd asked me a question during the pre-game show knowing I'd give him a long-winded answer, essentially buying time for him to get up to speed. So just to mess with him, I would give him a one-word answer to whatever question he asked. Marty and I had a lot of fun.

The Winter Meetings following the 1973 season were in Houston, and I was standing in the hotel lobby having a casual conversation with Dick Wagner, then assistant general manager of the Cincinnati Reds, and George Sisler, president of the International League. Wagner was in charge of having to hire a broadcaster for the Reds, who had recently lost the World Series to the Oakland A's.

Dick said, "Boy, I am so sick of listening to tapes. I must have listened to over 200 tapes and I am just sick of it."

I said, "I've got the best broadcaster around."

Wagner replied, "Really? Who's that?"

"A young guy named Marty Brennaman."

"Is he really that good?"

"Yes he is."

Wagner told me to have Brennaman send a tape to Cincinnati and have it on his desk by the time he returned from the Winter Meetings in a few days. Marty sent the tape and ended up on Wagner's short list for the job. The Reds flew Marty in to Cincinnati for an interview. Wagner, who was known for being a hard-nosed, tough guy, asked Marty, "What do you know about me?

Marty replied, "I know you're a ruthless son of a bitch."

Wagner responded with a line that has been re-told to me by both himself and Brennaman on separate occasions: "That f-ing Rosenfield!"

The Reds hired Marty for the 1974 season, and he has been the "Voice of the Reds" ever since. He was inducted into the broadcaster's wing in the Baseball Hall of Fame in 2000. Marty's son Thom joined him in the booth in 2010 and I thought that was really neat. When Marty was inducted into the Hall of Fame, he mentioned me. That was very, very nice. It's as close to the Hall of Fame as I'm ever going to get.

Pete Van Wieren had been the radio broadcaster of the games for the New York Yankees Double-A club, the Binghamton Triplets of the Eastern League in 1967 and 1968. He worked for the Triplets' radio station and was only around the team for the games. The franchise relocated after the 1968 season, leaving Van Wieren without a play-by-play job. It wasn't until the 1990s that minor league teams starting broadcasting games on a regular basis, so Van Wieren had slim-pickings if he wanted to stay in baseball.

He went to work for a television station in Toledo, but maintained his desire to get back into the play-by-play booth. I had met Pete once in 1973 when I went to Toledo to watch our club play the Mud Hens. While working at the television station, he saw over the wire service that Marty Brennaman had been hired by the Cincinnati Reds.

Pete called me from a pay phone and told me that he was interested in our play-by-play job. He was looking for a full-time job that included selling, doing appearances and being involved in the organization year-round. I was looking for someone who wanted to do those things as well. When Marty left, I listened to about a bazillion tapes. I liked everything about Pete's tape despite his lack of experience. So I gave him the job.

Pete broadcast the Tides for two seasons in 1974 and 1975, and did some writing for the *Ledger Star*, Tidewater's afternoon newspaper, as well. The *Star* was the sister newspaper to the *Virginian Pilot* and the *Star* did not send a writer on the road to cover the Tides. The *Pilot* sent George McClelland to cover the Tides home and away, and Pete would write stories about the Tides games for the *Star* to get the team more publicity.

After the 1975 season, George McClelland notified Pete that Milo Hamilton had been fired by the Braves and that there was an opening in Atlanta. They were looking for a broadcaster who worked year-round doing many of the same duties Pete had been fulfilling for us the past two seasons. The Braves hired Pete along with Skip Caray and Ernie Johnson. They would become national names thanks to Ted Turner's Superstation WTBS. Pete retired from Atlanta in 2008 and wrote his autobiography in 2010, entitled, *Of Mikes and Men*. There is a section in the book that Pete mentions me and the impact I had on his career.

I take a lot of pride in all of my employees, especially the broadcasters. Maybe it's because I had such an interest in that area. If I could help them get jobs at the next level, I would love to do that.

Image courtesy of Triumph Books LLC

Len Hathaway left the Tides and became the radio voice of the NFL's Washington Redskins. Larry Matson is now the broadcaster of the New Orleans Saints. Bob Socci has been doing Navy football and basketball in addition to the Tides.

Bob Rathbun ended up being a successor to Ernie Harwell in Detroit when he first left the Tigers in the early 1990s. Rathbun is now the voice of the NBA's Atlanta Hawks. When he worked in Tidewater in 1990, his partner in the booth was a guy named Ken Levine.

Ken Levine had spent the 1989 season broadcasting the Syracuse Sky Chiefs games in our league. That fall he sent his tapes out to a lot of clubs. I get a zillion tapes every year and after a while, they kind of all sound similar to some extent. But Levine's resume stood out to me. I looked it over and said to myself, "What is going on here? What's the story with this guy?"

Levine was a writer on television shows for the previous 20 years. He'd written episodes of "M*A*S*H," "The Jeffersons" and "Cheers." In fact, he'd won an Emmy for writing an episode of "Cheers." He was basically putting his Hollywood writing career on hold to pursue his real dream of being a Major League Baseball broadcaster. So I hired him to work with Rathbun.

While he was working for me, we became pretty good friends. During that time, he was writing an episode of "The Simpsons" and little did I know, he had a little surprise for me. He called me that fall and told me to watch this particular episode. I have to admit, I'm not a fan of "The Simpsons." Not that I don't like it, but I guess I've never really watched it. I watch a lot of television and love old re-runs and game shows. Anyway, Ken tells me to watch this show.

In this episode, Homer Simpson goes to the major leagues as a mascot for a team called the Capital City Goofballs. And he was terrible. And he gets called into the owner's office and they show him walking into the office. On the owner's door is a nameplate that reads DAVE ROSENFIELD. Homer goes into the office and the owner is just yelling and screaming at him and this guy fires Homer Simpson. It was pretty neat to see my name on the show. Even today, whenever that episode airs, I will get phone calls or emails from people telling me they saw it.

Incidentally, that episode of "The Simpsons" was the first time the team called the Springfield Isotopes was introduced as the town's professional baseball team. The Isotopes would be featured occasionally in various episodes over the years. In one particular episode in 2001, the Isotopes were threatening to move to Albuquerque. In real life around that same time, Tides president Ken Young was assembling a group to move a team to Albuquerque and that team ended up being called the Albuquerque Isotopes.

Ken Levine continued his writing career after his one year with the Tides. He worked on "Frasier," "Wings," "Everybody Loves Raymond," "Becker" and "Dharma & Greg." And he finally was able to fulfill his dream when he became a Major League announcer. He has worked for the Padres, Orioles and Mariners and also hosted pre-game and post-game shows for the Dodgers for three years.

But I digress. I was talking about our broadcasters.

We also employed Charlie Slowes, who is now the voice of the Washington Nationals. Charlie started out in the business at KMOX in St. Louis and he knew Bob Costas. One year, Charlie and I went to Spring Training in St. Petersburg. Charlie and I went over to Costas's condo that he was renting there and Charlie got Costas to record the audio for our opening and closing billboards, listing all of our sponsors. We had a list of like 30 sponsors. I remember Costas looking over at me and saying, "Do you have any play-by-play or is it all sponsors?" We used the opening and closing billboards with Bob Costas all year.

Another guy who I hired was Tony Mercurio. I hired him in 1977 to be our broadcaster and he worked for me for a while before we lost our radio deal. The new station we were getting our deal with made us hire a broadcaster from Michigan, so that left Tony without a job. I helped get him a job in Wichita that he kept for one season. He went to California and got involved in a woman's professional basketball league and he got involved in putting together some big rock concert out there. We always stayed in touch. He could sell.

This one particular year, I was looking to hire somebody for my office so I called him up and asked what he was doing. He said, "A little of this, a little of that. Why do you ask?"

I said, "Because I'm looking for somebody."

He said, "Do you know where there's a job?"

I said, "Yeah, about ten feet from here."

He said, "Yeah? Doing what?"

I said, "Selling, principally."

He said, "Well, yeah. I'd like to come back."

So I brought him back. He was basically my assistant. He sold and did a pretty good job. He didn't really want to broadcast again and I think he was doing the public address announcing. He was very outspoken about stuff he shouldn't get into. He was doing some part time radio stuff and he goes on the air just ripping Notre Dame. The station had a broadcast deal with Notre Dame at the time. One of our vice presidents was a Notre Dame guy and I ended up having to let him go again.

I helped him get a job at another radio station doing a one-hour sports talk show. I knew he'd be good at it because he's obnoxious. You have to be that way if it's going to work. You have to have people call up and say you're a jerk.

Blake Cullen had come into the picture by this time, which was like 1988 or 1989. Blake had asked me about him possibly getting involved in a minor league basketball team. I advised him, "Run, don't walk. Stay as far away from that as you can get." Blake called me later and asked me about hockey. I said, "Blake, I think it will work now." Cable television had exposed hockey to more people. Wayne

Gretzky had moved to Los Angeles. Hockey was high profile now and people were starting to talk about hockey again. Blake said he had a chance to get involved with the East Coast Hockey League and that he wanted to bring in an exhibition game just to see how it would work. I said, "Come on in and I'll do whatever I can to help you."

So we were sitting in my office and Blake said he needed somebody to help him with radio promotion and so forth. I told him I had the perfect guy for him, thinking of Mercurio. Tony loved hockey and was pretty knowledgeable about the sport. So I called Mercurio and Tony came over to the office. Blake ended up paying him some money to help him plus he bought some spots on the radio station.

Two teams that nobody ever heard of came in to play an exhibition game and drew like 6,000 people and now Blake was ready to go. The East Coast Hockey League wanted Norfolk so badly, they offered Blake a franchise here for zero.

A few days later, Bill Luther at The Scope arena called me and said, "I've got some stuff I've got to tell you. Your friend, Mr. Mercurio, has called me and wants to make a lease for hockey. He's going to try to get the East Coast Hockey League franchise in here."

I said, "*What?*"

I called the ECHL and Tony had already called them. The going price was $25,000 for a franchise and Tony offered them $25,000. So now, they were going to make Blake pay $25,000 when they were originally going to give it to him for nothing.

I called the radio station and told the station manager that I was coming over there and wanted him, Mercurio and anybody else he wanted present at that meeting. I was so damn mad, because I had brought him into this deal. I fired him again on the spot, and didn't speak to him again for eleven years.

My relationship with Mercurio is good now. It's been a joke that I fired him three or four times. I brought him back recently to be the second voice on our radio broadcasts again.

But I digress once again. My pride and interest in broadcasters goes back a long way. We've had some great broadcasters and I've always enjoyed my interactions with them and going on the air and doing the games with them. I have also really enjoyed my relationships with our managers over the years. None more so than with Frank Verdi.

Frank Verdi

CHAPTER TWELVE

FRIENDS AND COLLEAGUES

The 1977 season was around the corner and the Mets needed to hire a new field manager for the Tides. Nelson Burbrink, the Mets farm director, called me and asked, "Do you know any guys who are good managers who don't have a job?"

There was one guy who immediately came to my mind. "Yeah. He's out of baseball, but I think he might come back."

Burbrink said, "Who's that?"

"Frank Verdi."

Burbrink said, "Oh yeah. I know of him. You think he might come back? Why don't you call him and see what you can find out."

I had gotten to know Verdi when he was managing the Greensboro Yankees club back in the Carolina League in 1963. He was a veteran baseball manager who got one unofficial at bat as a Major Leaguer in his lone game with the New York Yankees. Verdi had managed in many International League cities – Syracuse, Toledo, Columbus and Rochester. He had played in Charleston and was very familiar with the IL. One home game against Syracuse in the 1970s was all I really needed to cement a relationship with him.

Syracuse was kicking our ass 12-0 in the top of the fifth inning. It started to rain and I told my groundskeeper to get lost. The umpire was calling for the tarp, and my grounds crew was nowhere to be found. The bottom fell out of the sky, and the game got rained out before it became an official game. The Met Park press box, where I could normally be found during a game, was five steps up the grandstand. I was sitting up there and Frank came running up those steps and opened the door of the press box, calling me names he was making up as he went along. Screaming and yelling and MF'ing me, calling me names, just making up stuff. One of Verdi's players was a fellow Italian named Frank Tepedino, who described Verdi's display of anger as "one hundred percent Italian."

During the following day's batting practice, Verdi was sitting in the dugout by himself. I walked down and sat down with him. I said, "Frank, you okay?"

He said, "Yeah, I'm fine. You know what ... about yesterday, I would have done the same thing."

So at the urging of Nelson Burbrink, I got a hold of Frank to see if Frank had any interest in coming to Norfolk to work for the Mets.

Frank said, "Ahh, shit. I got a good job. I'm happy. It'll screw me out of some money." Living on Long Island, Verdi was working at horse racing tracks around New York City. He was a Pinkerton security guard and a gambling nut. He'd gamble on anything. Verdi had either walked away or had gotten fired from jobs two or three times over $1500 in salary. He wanted $1500 and they wouldn't give it to him and he quit. Until he died, we'd laugh about that $1500. Frank said, "Yeah, I'll consider it." And 48 hours later, the deal was done and Frank Verdi became the manager of the Tides, and he was our manager for four seasons.

In the early days of Met Park, the city of Norfolk recommended that I hire a guy to be the head grounds keeper. The guy wasn't worth a shit and I had to let him go.

By this time, Whitey Herzog had become field manager of the Kansas City Royals. Herzog recommended a replacement, a guy named Smokey Olsen, who had been working as an assistant for George Toma. Toma was widely considered to be the guru of professional sports grounds keepers, having carved out an unparalleled 66-year career taking care of fields for the Kansas City Athletics and Royals, the World Series, the Super Bowl, the Olympics, soccer's World Cup and the list goes on. George said Smokey was going to be a great groundskeeper. So I hired him and everything was going to be the way George Toma did it, and it didn't matter what I wanted.

So Frank Verdi was managing our 1977 club. With the summertime heat and very little rain, the field would get so hard, Verdi and his players would complain about it. Every day, Verdi would say to Smokey, "You've got to put some water on the field. We have to soften it up. It's like a brickyard." And Smokey would throw three drops of water on it. Verdi would piss and moan to me about it.

One day, just prior to the beginning of batting practice in the early part of the afternoon, a batboy or someone came storming in to my office. The kid was almost hysterical. "Right now, you better come. Verdi wants you."

I rushed down to the field. Frank was sitting in the dugout and field was under water. It hadn't rained in days, and Smokey had flooded it. There was standing water on the infield. It was as if Smokey was sending a message to Verdi. "You want water on the field? *I'll give you water on the field!*" Verdi was going bananas. I said, "Frank, calm down. Somebody go get Smokey."

Finally Smokey came sauntering in to the dugout with this smirk on his face. I said, "Smokey, let me see your keys." Smokey handed me his keys. Then I said, "Now you've got fifteen minutes to be off this property. If I ever see you anywhere around here, I'll shoot you. Now get the hell out of my sight."

I took the keys, threw them to the 20-year old assistant grounds keeper Kenny Magner. Kenny started working for me five years earlier as a 15-year old. I said, "Kenny, it's all yours now."

And Kenny has been the head groundskeeper of the Tides ever since.

I guess we had a lot of stuff happen that year. I remember another story involving a guy, Art Clarkson, who worked for me for a short time. Art had been around in sports for a long time. He played a little bit of pro football in the Continental Football League. He had worked for former Tigers pitcher Denny McLain when McLain was the general manager of the Memphis club in our league back in the 1970s.

That's where I met Art. I hired him to come to Tidewater as my assistant in 1977.

Art was a hot-tempered guy. One night, there were two fans fighting in Met Park after the game was over. Art went down to try to break it up. He said, "Hey guys, let's take it outside." So they all walk outside the stadium. One of the guys punched him right in the mouth because he thought Art was challenging him.

After he left us, he was the guy who put together the deal to build a new ballpark, Hoover Metropolitan Stadium, in Birmingham, Alabama. He was the principal owner of the Birmingham club. He owned and ran a hockey team in Birmingham and is currently running an arena football team in Green Bay.

But I digress.

Frank Verdi was one of the most colorful characters I've ever known. Typical old time Italian – wife cooks and raises kids and has no rights and no privileges. His wife Pauline was a wonderful, wonderful woman.

Frank's wife and Mata were nearly inseparable due to the fact the Verdi never allowed his wife to drive a car. Mata was going to teach her how to drive once, and I thought Frank was going to kill her. Mata had to drive her everywhere during the season and the Verdi's always lived very close to us because of that. Mata took her to the store, the ballpark, everywhere because Frank wouldn't do any of it. She would bring her pasta maker every year. Frank and I would always have a couple of drinks after games and then we'd go to their apartment. There were all kinds of noodles everywhere, draped over chairs and couches. He had pasta practically every friggin' meal. We had really good times together.

Frank moved to Florida after he retired and we remained like brothers until he passed away in 2010. We'd talk on the phone watching the same game on television and we'd be making bets on what was happening in the game. Frank was just a fun guy. I probably stayed closer with him than with any manager I ever had.

We were both inducted into the International League Hall of Fame, appropriately enough, in 2008.

Frank Verdi receiving his International League Hall of Fame trophy from IL President Randy Mobley in 2008

I became good personal friends with people like Frank because we worked so closely together every day. I also became close with other people in the business that I didn't necessarily see as frequently. Like Frank Cashen.

Mrs. Payson passed away in 1975 and her family sold the Mets to Fred Wilpon and Nelson Doubleday in 1980. Upon taking over the franchise, the new ownership hired Frank Cashen to take over as the team's general manager.

As executive vice president in Baltimore, Frank had led the Orioles to World Series titles in 1966 and 1970. He left baseball for a short period of time to serve as vice president for the National Brewing Company and had most recently worked for Bowie Kuhn as Administrator of Baseball in the baseball commissioner's office. He was named to the Mets post in January 1980, and promised a five-year turn-around that was going to be focused primarily on building from within the Mets farm system.

Frank was the best executive I've ever been around by far. He's the most highly qualified person who's ever been in our business. There are no real *general* managers anymore. They are directors of player personnel now. Frank was a true *general* manager. Frank knew everything about business as well as the game. He was not just a guy who went to law school. He was a practicing attorney. He was a full-time sports writer. He ran a race track and helped run a brewery, in addition to running baseball teams. He was a guy who understood how to negotiate a television contract, ticketing, everything. He truly knew how to run a major league business, in addition to being a pretty astute judge of baseball players.

During Frank's visits to Norfolk, he'd spend countless hours in my office. We generally agreed on most things, but one thing bothered him. I drank out of the same coffee cup forever and never washed it. I'd rinse it, but someone told me once that not washing a coffee cup built up layers of taste in the ceramic. Frank always laughed about my coffee cup.

I used to spend a lot of time talking to players and I would try to help them in whatever way I could. And sometimes the promoter in me would come out and maybe the players could help me.

Mets executives (left to right) Al Harazin, Joe McIlvaine, and Frank Cashen hold up the 1986 World Series trophy after their Mets defeated the Boston Red Sox in seven games

I once had a guy who I thought we could really have a lot of fun with in terms of marketing him. He played for the Tides for three years from 1979-1981. His name – Ronald MacDonald. He was a pretty good player.

One of our real major sponsors was Burger King. I went to Charlie Broadwater, our regional guy with Burger King at the time, and told him, "I've got the greatest deal for you in history. Let's get Ronald MacDonald to do some television spots in his Tides uniform saying how much he loves eating at Burger King." This guy went crazy and thought it was the best idea in the world. The Burger King legal people would not allow him to do it. This guy had the name Ronald MacDonald long before McDonald's ever came up with that. But it never got done.

I couldn't help Ronald MacDonald, but that didn't stop me from wanting to help players or get involved with them and their careers.

There was a player named Bobby Brown in the mid 1970s that I'd gotten to know and kind of became a consultant for. He was from the eastern shore of Virginia and attended Northampton High School in Easton, located only about forty miles from Norfolk. Brown was drafted by the Baltimore Orioles in the eleventh round of the 1972 amateur draft. He played four minor league seasons with the Orioles. A pretty good hitter, the highest Brown ever played when he was with Baltimore was six games at Double-A in 1975.

Just prior to the start of the 1976 season, Baltimore released Bobby and he called me. I knew him, but didn't really know him well. He wanted a job in baseball, and he asked me for help. I told him I would call the Mets but not to expect much because I didn't have the power to do much. But I promised him that I would see what I could do to help.

The Mets said they didn't want to sign any players who had been released. I told them that Bobby was a pretty good hitter and he wasn't looking for much money. He'd go to Class A. He'd go wherever they wanted him to go. But the Mets weren't interested. So I called the Phillies. Paul Owens was now the general manager in Philadelphia.

Paul said they could use Bobby, so they signed him and sent him to Peninsula, which was in the Class A Carolina League. He went to Peninsula and hit about .360. The next year, the Phillies sent him to Triple-A in Oklahoma City and he did great there. They sent him back to Triple-A in 1978.

In June 1978, Bobby was traded along with Jay Johnstone to the New York Yankees in exchange for pitcher Rawly Eastwick, who the Phillies wanted to help bolster their bullpen during the pennant race. Bobby finished the year at Triple-A Tacoma and had certainly opened a lot eyes over the last few years.

I went to the Major League draft during the Winter Meetings after the 1978 season and I sat at the back of the room. They always have a microphone where teams would announce their selections. I hear, "With the first selection, the New York Mets select the contract of Rogers Brown from the Tacoma club." Here's a guy the Mets didn't want for three hundred dollars a month just three years earlier and now they took him in the Major League draft for $50,000."

Bobby bounced around from 1979 through 1982, playing in the Mets, Toronto, Yankees (again) and Seattle organizations, both at the major league and minor league levels with each club. He signed with the San Diego Padres for the 1983 season and had a decent year in a utility role shuttling back and forth between San Diego and Triple-A Las Vegas. Jack McKeon was the Padres General Manager.

McKeon and I were good friends. I got to know Jack when he was managing High Point in the Carolina League back in 1968. McKeon called me about Bobby before the 1984 season, which turned out to be the Padres' first division championship campaign in their history. "You've got to talk to your boy. He's holding out and he's not good enough to hold out. He's a utility guy and I love him, but he's not good enough to hold out. He's going to end up getting released if he's not careful. You've got to talk to him."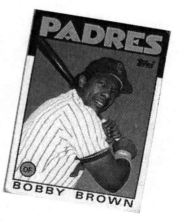

So I got a hold of Bobby and I told him exactly what Jack had said.

Brown said, "I'm better than that."

I said, "Bobby, you may think you're better than that, but that's the guy whose decision matters. Let's look at it another way. How much money do you need to live on? Can you live on $30,000?"

"Yeah, probably."

"Here's what let's do. Let's see if we can get them to give you $100,000. A two-year deal at $30,000 a year, the rest deferred. You start drawing it in say, five years. I think we could get Jack to give you that."

McKeon gave that contract to Bobby Brown.

I've got another McKeon story from back in the Carolina League days ...

Jack used to bring his young son Kasey along on road trips. Kasey was like five or six years old when his team came to Portsmouth to play us in 1968. The kid was walking around the outfield when our team was taking batting practice. He would tug on the pant legs of various players and would ask them all kinds of questions.

We had a guy named Billy Champion who pitched in the big leagues. Billy was a big, tall right-handed pitcher. The kid pulled on Champion's pants. "What's your name, red head?"

Billy looked down at this little kid and said, "Billy Champion."

"Oh. What do you do?"

Champion said, "I'm a pitcher."

The kid said, "What's your record?"

Billy said, "11 and 2."

The kid said, "Are you *shittin'* me?"

Jack told me later, "I don't think I'm going to be able to bring him on many road trips after this because he goes home and talks like how he hears everyone around the clubhouse talk."

But I digress.

I've had some real good people who have worked for me over the years. Not just broadcasters, but people in all sorts of roles.

Frank Viverito was my assistant GM in 1979-81. He's now the head of the sports commission for the city of St. Louis. While in Norfolk, Frank met his wife Patty, who was working for us as an account executive. Patty is now senior associate commissioner at the Missouri Valley Conference and is the only female commissioner of a major college football league.

There are way too many special people who have worked for me over the years for me to name all of them. Linda Waisanen started with me as a part time worker at the old ballpark. She became full time when we moved here and is our box office manager. She's been with me more almost 40 years.

Heather Harkins started at Harbor Park as an usherette when she was 16 in 1994 and worked her way into being a vital part of the operation. She is now our community relations director. Heather is a great kid. Her mother is a great lady – her mother's name is Mike. Dad's name is John. Wonderful family. She's married now and has the last name McKeating. She has a real cute son herself. She thinks I'm her grandfather or something. And the feeling is mutual. She's just very dedicated and has a very good feel for people.

R.C. Reutemann is like a son to me. He worked for me for eight years from 1984-1991 and I am as close to him as I am to anyone. The Mets needed someone to go run their Double-A club in Binghamton in 1992. He didn't want to leave me. I told him he had to take that job and if he didn't, I was going to fire him. He was ready for that job. He ended up going to Binghamton and then on to Brooklyn with the Mets and he did very well in both places.

RC Reuteman

I've mentioned Valerie Marshall a few times. She was with the Tides when I got here in 1962. What a character she was. Very outspoken and self-confident. And she was the reason that Mata and I moved to Virginia Beach.

We had been living in Chesapeake. Valerie's family ran a dairy about two blocks from where I lived. It was one of the last little independent dairies anywhere. They had like four cows and a couple of horses. One of her kids was real mischievous and was doing something to the horse and the horse bit her. It grabbed on to her arm and wouldn't let go. Valerie ends up biting the horse on the nose to make it let go of her daughter's arm.

Mata used to come to virtually every game. I would pick Valerie up in the morning and drive her to work. It was like a 40-minute ride from where we lived to Met Park. On non-game days, she'd ride home with me. On game days, she'd take my car home and then Mata and I would drive home together. Once Valerie couldn't work anymore, both Mata and I would have our cars at the stadium and both of us would have to make that long drive. It was just too far every night.

So that's what prompted us to move to Virginia Beach.

Sadly, Valerie got a malignant brain tumor in 1973 and that was the last year she worked with me. She died the next year.

FROM THE TIDES TO THE SHOW

Some notable Major League players and coaches
who have worn the Tides uniform over the years

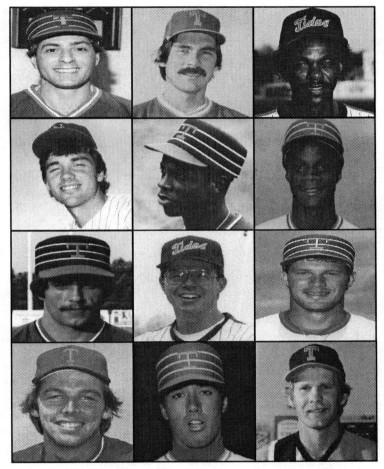

Top Row (L to R): Sam Perlozzo, Bruce Bochy, Ron Washington
Second Row (L to R): Billy Beane, Dwight Gooden, Darryl Strawberry
Third Row (L to R): Wally Backman, Mike Cubbage, Lenny Dykstra
Bottom Row (L to R): Ed Lynch, Ron Darling, Ron Gardenhire

FROM THE TIDES TO THE SHOW

Some notable Major League players and coaches
who have worn the Tides uniform over the years

Top Row (L to R): Jon Matlack, David Wright, Howard Johnson
Middle Row (L to R): Ned Yost, Jesse Orosco, Ruben Sierra
Bottom Row (L to R): Jason Isringhausen, Jose Reyes, Jose Lima

CHAPTER THIRTEEN

HOME IS WHERE THE HEART IS

We still live in Virginia Beach, but I really like the entire Hampton Roads community.

We loved Chesapeake also when we lived there. The city was newly formed in the late 1960s. I was approached to consider running for city council. I was pretty high profile at the time and well respected in that I was pretty outspoken about what I believed. I was flattered that somebody asked me, but I didn't have any money. It costs money to run for office. Also, I didn't know how much time I could really devote and still be able to do what I thought was important for my job. The group that approached me to run told me not to worry about the money and they said they would fund the campaign.

I said, "Gentlemen, I've got to tell you. I don't think you really want to do this. If you're going to fund my campaign, you're going to expect something from me. You're going to think that you can lead me to vote the way you want me to vote. But you're approaching me because you think I do what I believe to be right. And those two things are conflicting. If you want to fund this, and really want me to do that, you've got to understand that I'll be happy to listen to you. But I'm going to vote my conscience. I'd know no other way."

I think they were very appreciative that I did that, but that was kind of the end of my political career. That was really the only time I considered running for public office.

However, I did run for president of the National Association (known also as the "NA" or "Minor League

Baseball") in 1987. Johnny Johnson had been president for several years in the 1980s. The minor leagues were negotiating a new agreement with Major League Baseball during that time. A lot of people felt that I would do a good job representing the collective interests of the minor league operators. And many of us felt that the president needed to travel around and see the teams throughout the minors. I was pretty outspoken that we needed to have better representation of actual operators at the administrative level of the minor leagues.

I loved running a team and really had no interest in being a league president or being president of the NA. What I love about this game is being for something and to have to watch a game and be totally impartial would be very difficult for me. I would not have enjoyed it. I watch a Little League game and I find myself pulling for one of the teams. But this group of people convinced me to run, so I did.

This was in the summer of 1987. The election was coming up during the Winter Meetings in December. If I had won, we would have had to move to St. Petersburg right after the New Year. To try to sell a house when it was empty was something Mata wasn't going to do. So Mata and I decided to sell the house we lived in. Our plan was to purchase a lot. If I won the election, all we had to do was sell the lot. If I lost the election, we would build a house on the lot.

So we sold the house in the fall and we agreed to move out by December, one way or another. Mata and I loved Virginia Beach, and we drove around the area that we lived in looking for a place to rent. We looked at two or three different places and almost bought one. On a Wednesday, I saw this lot for sale. I thought it was a very nice lot and found out who owned it. On Friday, I made an offer, which they accepted. From the time starting in the summer and for the next few months, I designed our new house that we would live in if I lost the election.

I ended up losing the election, which was no great upset. In fact, I was very happy that we didn't have to move to Florida. I hate Florida. Summers there are intolerable. I also hate liver, which you already know. And, I also hate licorice. But I digress.

The election accomplished something that all of us wanted. The NA president was going to start travelling around seeing clubs across the country. We also changed the executive committee to where there was a league president and a club operator from each classification. I was on the executive committee for a long period of time until the current system was put in to place in the mid 1990s.

We ended up renting a house that we lived in for about five months as we built the house where I live now.

I have never really had any serious thoughts about relocating from the Tidewater area. I would have loved to have been a major league general manager, but I was never willing to do what it would take to get there. I would have had to take a very subordinate job and work my way up. Basically my whole time in baseball, I have had a wife and a kid. These jobs didn't pay anything. Lou Gorman, a dear friend, took the job as the assistant farm director in Baltimore for $450 a month. That was in 1962. I made $450 a month my first job in 1956. I couldn't do that with a wife and a kid.

The closest I ever got to ever came to getting a good big league job was in 1977.

A sportsman from Oklahoma, A. Ray Smith, owned minor league teams Tulsa, Louisville and New Orleans. Ray was putting together a deal to put a Major League Baseball team in New Orleans. (I was really good friends with Denzil Skinner, a guy who ran the Scope Arena in Norfolk when we built Met Park. Denzil had moved to New Orleans to run the

Superdome for the Hyatt Corporation and its chairman, Bob Pritzker. Because Hyatt was going to be involved in the loaning of the large sum of money to upgrade the Superdome for Major League Baseball, Pritzker was allowed to be involved in deciding who the general manager was going to be.)

I didn't have any idea that A. Ray was trying to put together this deal. The 1977 Winter Meetings were in Hawaii. I was walking through the lobby at the Sheraton Waikiki and I heard somebody shouting out my name. I turned around and it was Denzil Skinner. He came up to me, gave me a big hug, and said, "Do you want to be general manager of a Major League team? I might have a job for you." I had no idea he had anything to do with it. We spoke at length.

Mata and I were going to Maui after the meetings and so was Denzil so we decided to meet up for dinner on Maui. He took us to the Hyatt Regency on Maui, the most beautiful place I had ever been to in my life. Objects of art and black swans all over the place. Denzil and his wife, Mata and me, Bob Rathbun and his wife were with us and a guy who worked for Denzil actually running the Superdome also came along. It was the most expensive dinner I had even been to in my life. There were eight of us and the bill was in the thousands. It was unbelievable.

I was kind of walking on a cloud. If this thing was going to make this deal happen, I was in business. They had a meeting with all these guys that were going to invest in this Major League club in New Orleans. Franchises weren't valued as much as they are today. There were selling units at something like $200,000 apiece. Guys were verbally committing to various quantities of units, fifteen, maybe twenty, maybe another guy would take ten. Some guys were putting up some pretty good money. A. Ray Smith was the guy putting this deal together. They asked him how many units he wanted and he said, "I'll take two." The rest of the group was astonished. The meeting promptly broke up and that was the end of Major League Baseball in New Orleans.

That wasn't the only time I almost had an opportunity to go to work for A. Ray Smith. One of the teams he owned was the Louisville Redbirds, a Triple-A club in the American Association. At six o'clock one Sunday morning in 1982, Ray called me. I had no idea why he was calling me at that time of the morning. He said, "I want you to come be my general manager. I want you to come to work for me in Louisville."

I said, "Ray, I've got a good job. I'm well-settled here. Dick Davis is a great boss. I can pretty much do anything I want. He's a great guy to work for both personally and professionally. Why do I want to make a lateral move?"

He said, "I'll make it worth your while. Will you come and talk to me? Bring your wife, come to Louisville, and I'll show you around."

So Mata and I went to Louisville. He had this guy drive us around, showing us all over. He offered me a lot more money than I was making. I said, "Ray, I don't think so. I've gotten to know you pretty well over the years. You're going to want to be involved in every single thing I do. I'm going to say the Cap Night should be Tuesday and you're going to say it should be on Wednesday. That's no good for you and it's no good for me. You've always talked about going back to Oklahoma. When you decide you're going to permanently move back to Oklahoma but still own this club, you call me. I'll be happy to talk to you then. We're good friends. You're a smart, stubborn guy and I'm stubborn. I don't think me making this move makes any sense."

So I didn't go.

I really liked Norfolk and Virginia Beach and this whole area. I really liked my involvement in this community and wanted that to continue. There were a lot of good things we were doing for this community. Not only were we helping promote professional baseball here, we did a lot of things for kids and for amateur baseball as well.

A guy named Ed Nagourney, who was a huge baseball fan, was president of a local department store chain in Tidewater called Rices-Nachman. He and I had talked about doing something for kids and for Old Dominion University. We first did a small one-day clinic where we brought in Bud Harrelson at ODU in the late 1970s.

The next year, we started the Old Dominion Baseball Clinic. We did it every year in late January or early February. Years varied where we got six to ten major league players that would come. We had Hank Aaron, Brooks Robinson, Catfish Hunter, Harmon Killebrew, Cal Ripken, Dave Kingman. The "Who's Who" of who we had was pretty imposing. Just through friendships and relationships we were able to get all these guys.

We paid the players to come in, and Ed and I disagreed on how much we should pay them. Ed thought the bigger the name, the more he should get paid. I thought everyone should be paid the same amount. I didn't want us to be in the position of judging who the best was or who was a "big" name. We ended up giving everyone the standard deal – each player got $600 cash or we gave them a $1200 shopping spree at Rices-Nachman. We'd invite the players' wives to attend. Just before Spring Training, the wives weren't crazy about their husbands going off to do some clinic for three days in Norfolk, Virginia. We picked everybody up in limousines and took the players and their wives all to dinner on Saturday night.

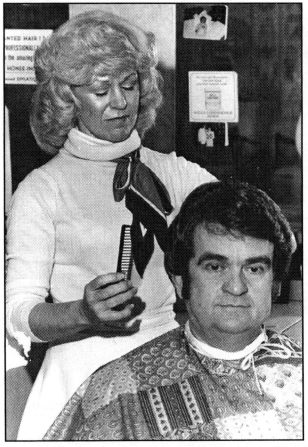

This photo was in a program ad for my hair salon in the 1980s

John Tudor did the clinic the year before he won the Cy Young Award, and then was delighted to come back when he was the reigning Cy Young winner.

Mookie Wilson

Mookie Wilson, who had played for us, did it for a few years and one year I didn't ask him to participate. I saw him at Spring Training and Mookie said to me, "Are you mad at me?"

I said, "No. Why would you think that?"

"Because you didn't ask me to do the clinic this year."

I said, "I didn't want to keep imposing on you."

I don't know if Mookie was offended that I didn't ask him, but he certainly made it clear that he loved doing it and wanted to come back again.

On Friday of the clinic weekend, we'd have a dinner for the players and sponsors and anyone else who was interested. Then on Saturday, we'd have two sessions of clinics with all the players we brought in plus some retired major leaguers from the area. The kids paid five dollars to participate and the parents could come and watch. We would bring in anywhere from 1,500 to 2,500 kids.

Bobby Brown (left) and Ken Singleton (right) with me during one of our dinners for the Old Dominion Baseball Clinic. I helped Bobby a bit with his career. Singleton had the best individual season a Tides player ever had.

In the ten years that I was involved, we raised approximately $400,000 for Old Dominion baseball. It was significant enough that Old Dominion was able to get some funding to build their baseball park. Their park is named for Bud Metheny, who was the long-time coach and athletic director at ODU. He was the player who played right field for the Yankees after Babe Ruth. Bud was also a graduate of the College of William & Mary and a long-time resident here. They were able to build the field that is named for him, and that was very gratifying to be a part of that. It was fun and great for the kids to be able to see these guys. The money that was raised through the sponsorships and through the registrations was significant in getting a lot of kids to go to ODU and play baseball.

Being a part of the community is something that has been important to me.

I've been involved in the Norfolk Sports Club since I came here in 1962, even though I lived in Portsmouth and we were kind of the illegitimate children in the area. For years, the Norfolk Sports Club's weekly meetings were held in the restaurant at Met Park. The Norfolk Sports  Club has a huge dinner that raises scholarship funds for high school athletes. I was honored once as their Sportsman of the Year.

I've also been involved to a lesser degree with the Virginia Beach Sports Club.

I've been involved with the Chamber of Commerce. We did something that's been beneficial. Sometime in the early 1990s, American Movie Classics did a thing called "Diamonds on the Silver Screen" where they showed a bunch of baseball movies. The local cable provider wanted to get involved somehow with that. So they approached us and put on a dinner. I got Catfish Hunter, John Stearns and Ed Kranepool to come to that dinner. The movie I was almost in when I was a kid, "The Pride of the Yankees," was shown at one of the local theaters as a fund-raiser. We raised a bunch of money through sponsorships and we created something called the Youth Baseball Fund, which is still going.

Every youth baseball organization in the world needs money, particularly when it comes to their champion going on to a regional or some travelling tournament. We came up with the idea that those teams that have to travel out of the area would each receive $200 from this fund to help with their expenses. The Tides would match that amount, so these teams were guaranteed to receive $400.

We have a deal on our concourse at Harbor Park where fans can contribute to that if they want and that helps keep that fund going. In the International League, we receive a share of the fine money that is collected throughout each season. We contribute our share to the Youth Baseball Fund. The fund has gotten a little thin, but at least we've been able to do something.

But I digress. Once I helped a player with a little fund raising of his own. True story.

Charlie Howard was a player for the Pittsburgh Pirates Triple-A affiliate, the Charleston Charlies, in the early 1970s. Charleston was in Tidewater during the final few days of the 1972 season playing against the Tides. Somehow along the way, I had gotten to know him a little bit.

Charlie had this great Fu Manchu mustache. Harding Peterson, the Pirates farm director, was in town at the time. The Pirates, like many organizations, prohibited their minor league players from having any growth of facial hair. Peterson said, "Charlie, you've got to shave that thing. You know our policy about facial hair. If you don't shave that mustache, it's going to cost you fifty bucks."

So I was sitting in the Charleston dugout during batting practice, joking around with some players and their field manager. Charlie Howard entered the dugout and proceeded to tell the group that he was told to shave.

I said to him, "You want to have some fun?"

Charlie said, "Doing what?"

I said, "Why don't you only shave half of it and hand him twenty five dollars?"

And he did.

And speaking of mustaches, I've got another mustache story. Sometime in the 1970s, I wanted to see if I could grow a mustache. So I grew a pretty good one but I really wanted to get rid of it. It itched and was kind of a pain. Mata kept after me to shave it, so naturally I resisted.

I made a pact with myself. If she ever went two weeks without nagging me about it, then I was going to shave it. I wasn't going to give anyone the satisfaction of *making* me shave it. She'd go nine days, then six days and then twelve days. I kept thinking "if she could only go two more days…" She said I looked like Captain Kangaroo.

So finally, the two-week mark ended up being on a Saturday morning. We were sitting having breakfast and I got up, went in to the bathroom and finally shaved the damn thing. I came back into the kitchen and she was kind of stunned. She said, "What prompted that?"

I said, "Because you didn't nag me about it for fourteen days!"

But I digress.

Like I was saying earlier, there are so many special people who I've worked with over the years.

And not only have I been around some great people, I've been fortunate to be around some pretty neat events in baseball history. I was in the LA Coliseum when the Dodgers played the Giants in the first game ever played there when Major League Baseball expanded to the west coast in 1958. I went to the 1966 World Series in Baltimore.

And then there was 1986. That season, the Mets brought all of their minor league general managers to Shea

Stadium to work in a variety of roles during the playoffs against Houston Astros and the World Series against the Boston Red Sox.

Frank Cashen and Al Harazin, his assistant general manager, knew they could assign me a couple of particular jobs that I'd do well. I was in charge of the field gate behind home plate before the game and I had to only allow people onto the field if they had certain credentials. Frank and Al knew I would do whatever was necessary to keep people off the field that didn't belong there.

During the game, my job was to be in charge of the auxiliary press box, which was adjacent to the Diamond Club at Shea Stadium. Some of the chefs and other people were used to using that entrance to get into the press box. Regular Mets employees never told them "no" because they were probably getting fed for free. It was up to me to enforce the rules, but it was a very fun thing to do. It really made you feel you were a part of a major event.

And when the ball got through Bill Buckner in game six of the World Series, I was right there in the Shea Stadium auxiliary press box, screaming and shouting like the rest of the 55,000 people who witnessed one of the most remarkable games in baseball history. Of course, the Mets went on to defeat the Red Sox in game seven, winning their first World Series since 1969.

Another digression.

Mata and I went to New York at the end of the 1982 season to watch the Mets play. We were in this hotel, the phone rang and it was Jack McKeon calling from San Francisco. Somehow he had tracked me down. "Dave, we've got a real problem."

I said, "What's the problem?"

Clyde McCullough was a coach for the San Diego Padres at the time. Jack said, "We just found Clyde dead in his hotel room. He had a heart attack. I need you to be the one to tell Ann." Clyde's wife Ann was at home in Virginia Beach.

I said, "Jack, I'm in New York."

Jack said, "Well, it has to be done quickly because we're playing on national television this afternoon and I'm not going to be able to keep it quiet." The Padres were in San Francisco playing the Giants and the game was going to be on the NBC "Game of the Week" telecast in just a few hours. "I can't let Ann hear about this on television."

I told him that even though I couldn't get back to Norfolk before the telecast started, I had two guys back home who knew Clyde very, very well – a scout named Harry Postove and Ray White, another baseball guy for years. I called Postove and White and asked them to go tell Ann McCullough that her husband had passed away.

I told Jack, "We'll head back to Norfolk right now. I'll get there as fast as I can." Mata and I sped back to Norfolk and immediately went to the McCullough home to join up with a pretty distraught family. We didn't know how to plan a funeral or anything else. They asked me to take charge of it.

They asked me to do the eulogy. I had never done anything like that before, but said okay. We set the funeral up, who was coming, a lot of clubs sent people. All kinds of people. I really loved Clyde. He was a strange guy, but he and I had a lot of fun. I did the eulogy, which was very difficult. People were crying, and I was crying. I got finished, and his daughter threw herself into the casket, trying to hug him, and I was trying to pull her out of the casket. It was the god damnest thing. Unbelievable. What do you do? People were just aghast at this whole scene. It was unbelievable.

Clyde had been one of my favorite managers and we were pretty close. It was easier for me to get close to managers for a lot of reasons. Bobby Valentine and Davey Johnson are the two best managers I ever had in terms of managing the game. Bobby and I are very close to this day. Sam Perlozzo and Rick Dempsey are on that list too.

Bobby Valentine (top left), Rick Dempsey (top right), and Davey Johnson (bottom)

I've been close to several colleagues in the International League and around the baseball world who have become very good friends as well. I was very fond of George Sisler, who was the general manager of three different clubs in our league and ultimately became president. I used to drink pretty hard with Gene Cook, who was the GM in Toledo for 20 years. I've been close with Tex Simone from Syracuse forever. Of the group now, I'm very friendly with and close to Ken Schnacke in Columbus and Mike Tamburro and Lou Schwechheimer from Pawtucket. I think the world of Randy Mobley, who has been the president of the International League since 1990. He and I are as different as chalk and cheese, but if I need help with a huge problem, Randy's the guy I think of. In every case of people whom I'm close to, it's because I have a lot of respect for them and I think they are good, decent people. I think they have the same view of integrity as I do.

Randy Mobley presenting me with my IL Hall of Fame trophy in 2008

Back in the day, I used to get pretty close with players as well. We had some great players, but that didn't mean I was necessarily close with those guys. In fact, Ken Singleton was the greatest single player I've seen in a Tides uniform. He only played in 64 games with us in 1970, but he hit .388 with 17 home runs and had 46 runs batted in during that stint. He wasn't with us long enough for me to get to know him real well. I think the world of Mike Cubbage and Ron Gardenhire, who played for us in the early 1980s. In recent years, I haven't been as involved with or as close to players as I used to be.

But one guy who is top of my list as far as being like family to me is a kid named Clint Hurdle ...

Clint Hurdle circa 1983

Clint Hurdle was widely viewed in baseball circles as a can't-miss prospect with Kansas City after the Royals selected him with their first round pick in the 1975 amateur draft. In fact, *Sports Illustrated* labeled Hurdle as a "phenom" on their magazine's cover in 1978. His playing career didn't quite live up to the jinxing prediction made by *Sports Illustrated.* He had been released by Seattle at the end of Spring Training in 1983. Hurdle signed with the Mets to go to Triple-A as a designated hitter. The International League played with American League rules part of the time, which meant he was going to be a part-time player without a position.

Davey Johnson was our manager. He pulled Hurdle into his office when Clint arrived and told him he was starting here with a blank slate. Davey told Clint that he had heard a lot of things about him, but none of that mattered. He was going to do his best to get Hurdle as much playing time as he could. I spent a lot of time talking to Clint also. We just hit it off from the beginning. I guess we were kind of kindred spirits. We just had a bond.

Clint bounced back and forth between the big leagues and the minors for the next few seasons. He played with us for parts of a couple of years in 1983 and 1984 and then came back in 1987. By the end of the 1987 season, Hurdle had discussed a post-playing career as a manager with Mets farm director Steve Schryver. Initially, Schryver had indicated that there would be an opportunity for Hurdle to manage the Mets rookie club in Sarasota, on the west coast of Florida. Hurdle did want to manage, but he preferred to manage the Mets Class A club in St. Lucie, which was only about 35 miles from his home on the east side of the state.

Clint and I would talk about him continuing his playing career or potentially becoming a coach or manager. We talked a lot. He ended up managing starting in 1988 and moved his way up in the Mets system. Four years after he stopped playing, Clint came back to the Tides for the 1992 season, but this time as our field manager.

That's really when we became very, very close. We were going through a lot as an organization at that time. We were building Harbor Park, which was kind of like starting a new franchise in a lot of ways. Both Clint and I had a lot going on in our personal lives as well. There wasn't anything we didn't talk about. We went through a lot of stuff together.

I still speak to Clint pretty frequently. When he was managing in Colorado and after he got the managerial job in Pittsburgh, we'd talk about potential coaches for his staffs. I'm very proud of what he's accomplished and how he's evolved. He's like a son to me.

CHAPTER FOURTEEN

AN AWAKENING

Speaking of sons, I digress again.

For no particular reason, I haven't mentioned Marc a whole lot.

We're just two entirely different people. Our interests have never been the same. Maybe it's kind of a rebellion on his part, I don't know. I've never liked fishing and he'd rather fish than eat. I'm not big with music and he fools around with music. He's a guy that likes to work out and he does some personal training. He learned a lot from me about a work ethic and he's a good, honest, decent person. He and I have never been crossways with each other, but we've never quite been on the same wavelength.

I admit that I wasn't the best father to Marc. I worked too much. I never really wanted more children. I spent so much time working that I'm not sure how fair it would have been to have more kids. I often kiddingly said that one child is somewhere between just the right amount and one too many.

He's been a good husband and a good father and a decent guy. I think he's had a happy life and has been a hard-working guy. The people he's worked for have always said he's been a good worker. Marc worked on the Tides grounds crew for a while before leaving to go to work for the City of Norfolk. He was in charge of Town Point Park, which is located fairly close to Harbor Park. After doing that for a few years, Marc went to be in charge of a big soccer complex in Virginia Beach and he was also in charge of the grounds at a private school. Marc currently works for a Navy subcontractor in Norfolk with the responsibility of doing away with all the vegetation from around giant fuel tanks. I find that ironic because he has studied so much about how to grow all kinds of plants and now his job is to kill this stuff.

We have never been real close, yet I have always loved him. And I know he loves me. Over the years, I've learned to tell him that I love him. We didn't have a lot of "I love you" when he was younger. A combination of two very significant things in my life taught me how to tell him that I love him and how important that is.

Marc with his daughter Keren in 1988

One of these was very sad but very impactful on me …

Mata and I were supposed to be going to the final playoff game for the Admirals in 1991. Mata really liked hockey and we went to almost all the games. When I called her and told her what time I was going to pick her up and she said, "I don't know if I want to go. I've had a blinding headache. It's gone right now but I'm not feeling very good."

I said, "Well, I won't go."

Mata insisted. "You go ahead, I'll be fine."

I called her again before I went. She still said she wasn't feeling very well. The headache was gone. And I called her again in the middle of the game and she still didn't feel good, so I left. I didn't see the end of the game. I went home. Mata started feeling better for about three or four days.

The Tides had an exhibition game, or it was Opening Day. I don't remember. I got up in the morning and she said some things that were totally out of character. Marc was living with, and would ultimately marry, Betsy, a gal who was finishing nursing school. I called her and said, "I can't stay home. Are you free today?"

She said, "Yeah."

"Can you come and stay with Mata and see if you think we need to get her to a doctor? I'm concerned. You can probably tell a lot better than I can whether or not we need to get her to a doctor."

Betsy came to the house and I left for the ballpark. A short while later, Betsy phoned me at the office and said, "Dave, I think we need to get her to the doctor."

I called Mata's physician who agreed to see her. I described what was going on and the doctor said, "Why don't I meet you at the hospital?"

I called Betsy and told her to get Mata dressed and that I'd be right home. Upon arriving at the house, Mata said,

"I'm not going to the doctor. I know myself. I don't need the doctor."

I said, "You're *going* to the doctor."

She insisted, "*No*, I'm not."

So I called 9-1-1 and got an ambulance to come and take her to the hospital.

Upon our arrival, the doctor got a neurosurgeon to help examine Mata. The surgeon told me that Mata had an aneurysm that had burst and apparently had stopped bleeding. The doctor said, "It's pretty serious. Within 24 hours, she will probably go into a coma. That is the natural progression of this. We'll have to wait and see what happens. We may have to do surgery. But we'll have to wait and see."

By the next day, Mata had slipped into a coma. The doctors performed some physical therapy so that Mata's muscles didn't atrophy. The doctors told me that the area of her brain that had been affected was the speech center.

"If it's just the speech, we can handle that," said the doctor. He explained that there is a second speech center that, if affected, makes it difficult for a person to recognize speech and makes living a decent life nearly impossible because of the inability to fathom what's happening around them.

I was at the hospital on and off several times a day. She was in the hospital for three weeks. Our 35th wedding anniversary was when she was in the hospital. One day I got a call at five o'clock in the morning. She had another aneurysm.

Marc and I rushed back to the hospital where we were told that Mata's chances of surviving were possibly five percent, and that the chances she would experience a meaningful recovery were probably less than that. My grave concern was what Marc's reaction would be. I had visions of him saying, "This is my mother. I'll take care of her forever." He wasn't aware of the conversations she and I had had regarding wanting to live a quality life. Marc looked at me and said, "Dad, we have to let her go. She wouldn't want this." I knew that's what had to be done.

I said, "Marc, I'm so grateful that we agree."

We took the life support away. She passed very peacefully a couple of hours later.

The day of Mata's funeral coincided with the day of Betsy's graduation from nursing school. Betsy told me, "I don't think I can go through with my graduation without her."

I said, "Betsy, that's why you've *got* to do it. It's kind of like she's passing you the torch." And with a heavy heart, Betsy graduated from nursing school.

I mentioned earlier that Mata's death played a major role in how I viewed my relationship with Marc. I had a huge awakening when Mata died.

It had never dawned on me that I could be left alone. I was seven or eight years older than she was and she took great care of herself. I never did. We used to talk about what she would do when I was gone. I wanted her to be happy. I had said to her, "If you want to have a date at my funeral, its fine with me." I was sure I was going to die before her. But to all of a sudden be left alone? There are certain things you never think about and that one had never crossed my mind. It was very hard on me. I had never thought about my own mortality. I was sixty-two years old. I should have thought about that at some point, but I never did. Not necessarily worrying about it, but it should have at least occurred to me.

Mata's death was the shock of my life. I started to understand how fragile life is.

A lot of people called and sent their cards. I was numb. Mata and I were married for thirty five years. What was I to do? I am not the type of person who feels sorry for myself, but this was something I just wasn't prepared for.

Before Mata passed away, I had promised her I would lose weight. I made her that promise having no idea what was going to happen to her, but I didn't do anything about it until she died. I ended up going on Nutrisystem and lost about one hundred and ten pounds. I was pleased that I kept that promise to her.

After Mata died, I wasn't interested in anything. I was very distraught. Finding someone else was the farthest thing on my mind.

CHAPTER FIFTEEN

CHARMAINE

Charmaine Barger and I had been friends since the time that she handled all the Tides airline travel through a local travel agency. She had left the agency and I had only seen her once or twice in the previous 15 or so years.

She had read in the newspaper that Mata had passed away and called to offer her condolences. She is an enormously compassionate person who truly understands people. She told me, "I know what a difficult time this must be for you and often it is easier to talk to a stranger than it is to talk to a friend who may be a constant reminder of your loss."

How right she was. After a few months, I decided to call her. I used to know her pretty well, but quite a number of years had passed since we last really knew each other. When we worked together several years prior, I would go to the travel agency to pick up airline tickets. Charmaine's daughter Samantha would often be there on weekends, coloring and otherwise involved with activities to keep busy while her mother worked. I always remembered her name because Mata and I had owned a female boxer named Sam. I didn't tell Charm that right away. When Charm called me, I said, "How's Sam?"

Charm said, "I can't believe you remember her name."

I said, "How old is she? What grade is she in now?" I thought she was possibly in high school.

She said, "Dave, I think it's been longer than you think. She's a junior at Old Dominion University, majoring in Engineering."

When I first called her, I was on the Triple-A expansion and realignment committee. Triple-A Baseball was preparing to expand by two clubs to correspond with the Major Leagues adding Florida and Colorado in 1993. We had to go and travel to different places and look at different cities. I think we had gone to Ottawa, I can't remember. We were coming back on a Friday night, the team was on the road, and I had nothing to do.

If I got together with any of my friends, all they were going to want to do was talk about Mata and it was pretty painful. I really just needed to get away, and I didn't know what to do, so I called her at work from an airport in Pittsburgh or Philadelphia or someplace and asked her if she'd like to get together for dinner on the weekend. And she said, "Fine." We were going to get together on Saturday.

Once on the airplane heading home, I realized that I hadn't set a time for our dinner, and I didn't know her home telephone number. I didn't know anything. It really hadn't occurred to me. Not having dated in 35 years, I wasn't too good at it. When you haven't dated in forever, it was really difficult. Horribly difficult. I felt like I was getting zits popping on my face. Having grown up around six sisters, I was not very good with ladies. All I wanted to do was play baseball. I didn't dance well. I could talk to girls pretty well, but as far as dating, I was not big.

I woke up on Saturday morning. I said to myself, "*Shit!* I don't know where she lives. I don't know how to get a hold of her. I sure as hell hope she's working."

I called her office and she was not working. I started calling anybody I thought might know her, trying to find out how to get a hold of her. I looked her up in the phone book. No listing for her. I start calling people, and I know people probably thought I was nuts. The people who knew her number weren't about to give it to me. They thought I was some lunatic. And I was getting more and more nervous. I thought, "Boy, I've really screwed this deal up."

I knew Howard Jacobson, one of the owners of the agency where Charmaine worked. I looked up Jacobson's home number in the phone book and found three people with the same name and called each one. Naturally, the last one I reached was the right one. I'm leaving messages all over the place. So, finally around one o'clock, she finally called me. She said, "I don't know what else you are, but you are some kind of persistent! I was getting calls from all over the place that you were trying to reach me."

Charmaine said that she had to go to a wedding that afternoon, which just happened to be near my house. I gave her my address and phone number. She said, "I'll just come by your house afterwards, and we'll go from there."

We were friends but I thought to myself, "She's not giving me her phone number or her address, so that way if she's not happy with this whole thing, she can get rid of me real easy." From that thinking, you can tell that I hadn't dated for 35 years and was pretty unsure of myself.

And I sat at home and waited and waited, and was getting more and more nervous by the minute. It was like I was back in high school. She finally showed up, and the funny thing, it was good that she came to the house, because if I had to meet her somewhere, I wouldn't have recognized her. Anyway, she walked in the door, gave me a kiss on the cheek and we had a drink, went out to dinner and we just started spending time together.

At one point (I'm not certain how long we'd been seeing each other at this point), we'd been out one night. I walked her to the door and into the foyer and kissed her good night. And I started laughing. She said, "That's real nice. What's so funny?"

I said, "If I'm not married in three weeks, I don't even know how to make a good pass."

I was sure of my feeling for Charmaine. I first addressed the topic of marriage to her in about October, about four months after we started dating. Charmaine said, "I know how I feel, but I don't know about you. We'll keep seeing each other and when I'm convinced that you know what you're doing, we'll talk about it."

About another month had passed when she said to me, "I think you know what you're doing. If you still want to marry me, I'll marry you."

She had been married previously for five years, to Stan Barger, an instructor at Tidewater Community College. (I have a good relationship with Stan. I call him my "husband-in-law.") But she had been single for more than 20 years. She finally dropped her standards a little bit.

We wanted to get married in front of a big roaring fireplace. We decided to get married at this restaurant that I always loved. It was an old house that a guy made into a restaurant. If someone had told me when I finished my freshman year in college that I was going to marry a girl who hadn't been born yet, I wouldn't have believed that. Charmaine was born shortly after my freshman year at UCLA. We were married on February 1, 1992.

I've been really fortunate. They say you're lucky if you have one good spouse. And I've had two very good ones. And I don't think I've been a great husband. The fact that

Mata and Charmaine are both very different from each other is better because I don't make a lot of comparisons. They are just two totally different people. One marriage lasted a year and a half, but I don't really count that one. The next one lasted 35 years. And this one has lasted 20, *so far*. Not a bad average.

Charmaine is one of 10 children, two of whom died very early in life. She grew up as one of eight children, six girls and two boys – just like me. Charmaine's birthday is one day before mine. And Mata and Stan Barger shared birthdays one day apart. Kind of ironic. Maybe we were destined to be together.

Charm is such a kind person. She's never met a stranger. She'll tell people that she's shy. Yeah, *right!!* The first time I took her to a baseball gathering was a Triple-A meeting in Palm Springs. She told me to go see my friends and that she'd be fine. She said, "You don't have to babysit me." And in about a half an hour, she knew about half the people around. She is *not* shy.

It's nothing for Charm to be taking a walk around the neighborhood and go to someone she doesn't know to tell them how much she likes their garden or their flowers. She is just a very nice person.

The advent of Charm was the other major factor in me realizing that I needed to be a different kind of person myself. Her influence on me has been significant in showing and telling people who I care for how I feel about them.

Charm and me during our honeymoon

Particularly Marc. I always thought it was just understood. I thought, "He's my son. He knows that I love him." Maybe that's okay for me, but a lot of people need to hear that and to have that reassurance.

Marc has been a good father. He and Betsy have three daughters – Amy, Holly and Keren. Charm's daughter Samantha has a young boy named Jake. I like spending time with the kids and the grandkids and I have two great-grandchildren as well. We also spend a lot of time with Charm's family, which is really neat for me. I can honestly say that family is much more important to me than it was earlier in my life.

But I digress. Whew.

The Rosenfield siblings celebrating my brother's 90th birthday in 2001 (from left to right - me, Mary, Dellie, Leon, Julie and Nancy)

CHAPTER SIXTEEN

A WHOLE NEW BALL GAME

Frank Cashen was the Mets Chief Operating Officer when the Tides' new ballpark project was getting underway. Al Harazin was the general manager. Frank and Al met with Dick Davis and me at Spring Training in 1991. They told us that the Mets ownership wanted to sell both our franchise and their Double-A franchise in Binghamton. They said, "We both are opposed to it, particularly with the new ballpark coming in downtown. We think it's going to be a great franchise, but the Mets ownership wants to divest of those two assets."

They asked Dick Davis, "Do you think your group would want to buy the team?"

Dick said, "How much money are you talking about?"

Frank said, "Probably about seven million."

Dick said, "No way. Our board is all old. We're not going to go and try to sell stock again. I don't see any way we can do that."

So Frank said, "We are asking you to keep this completely confidential. We don't want everybody coming in kicking tires, looking at the financials. We're going to sell it, but we're going to do it very quietly. We're asking you not to tell anybody, including your own board."

This really presented a problem. In my mind, when somebody tells me something and pledges me to secrecy, I have no question that's what I've got to do. But Dick Davis felt a strong obligation to tell the board.

I said, "Dick, you're the president. You do whatever you think you gotta do. I'm not telling anyone, because I gave them my word." So, Dick and I decided that we were going to keep the news to ourselves.

It was now 1992 and the construction on what would become Harbor Park had begun. We were working with Bill Luther of the City of Norfolk as well as with the Mets.

I had been in the process of negotiating concessions contracts for the new stadium. I'd spoken with Volume Services and several other companies. Frank Cashen asked me whom I had spoken to and I told him. Frank said, "There's somebody else I'd like you to talk to. This guy ran the concessions when we were in Baltimore. His name is Ken Young and his partner is a guy named Vince Pantuso. We found them to be very good operators and good people and I'd like you to talk to them."

I said, "Fine."

So, Ken and Vince came up to talk to me. And I flew to Orlando to look at their concessions operation at the Orlando Arena where the NBA's Magic played. They had some neat ideas. Ken and I agreed on the parameters for a food service deal at the new ballpark. Their company was going to be the concessionaire at Harbor Park.

During Spring Training in March 1992, Ken drove over to Port St. Lucie from Tampa where he lived. Ken, Al and I were standing on the field in Port St. Lucie talking. Al said, "Okay Ken, I understand that you and Dave have just about reached a deal on the concessions at the new ballpark."

Ken said, "Yes."

Al said, "Well, there's a couple of things I need to tell you. You might not be working with Dave and you might not be working with the Mets."

Ken said, "What do you mean?"

Al said, "The Mets ownership wants to sell this franchise and whoever buys it may not want to work with the Mets and whoever buys it may not want Dave to be the general manager."

Ken said, "Are you really going to sell it?"

Al said, "Yes. But, we're not talking about it publicly."

Ken said, "I've been a fan all my life. I may try to put a group together to buy it."

A couple of weeks later, Ken called him back and said, "Okay, let's talk about it. Let's see what we can do."

Late in the 1992 season, Al Harazin came to Norfolk and spoke to the board of Tidewater Professional Sports (TPS). It was at that meeting that Al informed the board that the Mets were selling the team. It was a complete and total shock to them that this was happening. They were absolutely irate at me and at Dick for not having told them. They fired me on the spot and totally ostracized Dick.

With the fiscal year set to end September 30, and the partnership between the Mets and TPS terminating, all the business affairs had to be finished, so I went on the Mets payroll to close everything down. The framework of the deal with Ken Young was now in place and he went about getting his investors in place and took nominal charge until his group finally closed the following May.

From the public's perception, there was never any lull in the operation. The board was very upset and that was the impetus to get Dick Davis out of the group. Dick was close to retiring anyway. They were upset with me. They didn't know Ken. They didn't think they wanted anything to do with the club after it was all over. But they had a fair amount of money. It took several meetings with Al Abiouness, the TPS Vice President and several board members, before they eventually felt comfortable and joined the group. They have continued to participate and been great supporters over the last 20 years.

TPS hired a CPA firm to do an audit. I think they thought they'd find something very wrong with our operation. I don't know what the hell they thought. This CPA firm came in and did as thorough an audit as you've ever seen in your life and reported back to them that it was the best-kept financial records they'd ever seen.

One of the auditors also represented a guy named Mark Garcea, who was a wealthy guy, but nobody ever heard of him. He was interested in doing something to elevate his stature in the community. And he became one of the first investors with Ken.

By early 1993, Ken Young had assembled a group to purchase the Tidewater Tides from the Mets for $7.1 million and a new era of ownership was underway.

Ken Young

We moved in to Harbor Park and changed our name to the Norfolk Tides, which I admit is still sometimes difficult to say even after twenty years.

I remember a side story from the first season in Harbor Park. The Mets asked Major League Baseball to come up with a new primary logo for us. It was a blue "T" with a wave forming the line on top of the letter (and is still the team's primary logo today). We started using the new logo, and we got a cease and desist letter from Nike saying that our logo looked too much like their "swoosh." We never modified the logo and kept talking to them about it, and finally they just said "okay" and they went away.

But I digress.

I didn't know how Ken and I were going to get along. Here was a guy who had never been involved in owning a team. I didn't know if he was going to like me or if I was going to like him and I wasn't used to a guy who wanted to be in the middle of everything. We sat down one day to talk. Ken said, "People tell me that you're as good a general manager as there is around. You don't know me and I don't know you. Why don't we shake hands on a two-year deal? And after two years, we'll sit down and see how we like each other.

I said, "Okay."

The only written employment contract I ever had in my life was 1961 in Topeka, and that's when I got screwed. So Ken's handshake was good enough for me.

Ken and I were having a beer together at the 1993 Winter Meetings in Louisville after Ken's first season as the new owner. He said, "Remember our conversation about two years? Well, forget about it. Work as long as you want."

And two decades later, we are still together. Ken has let me run the club as if it was my own, much like Dick Davis and the Mets did before him. He's certainly been more involved, but he has so many other business interests, he can't be in Norfolk all the time.

Ken has let me be who I am without trying to change me. He has respected my style and my way of running a club. I have learned a lot from him as well. He has taught me a lot about customer service and he likes a lot of the entertainment stuff that Pat Williams used to talk about. Ken is the president of the club and I never represent myself as the owner, even though I still operate as if it's my own money. We certainly have worked together on some major decisions.

Probably no decision was bigger than what we went through in 2006 when we split up with the Mets after 38 years.

Allow me to explain …

Harbor Park

CHAPTER SEVENTEEN

THE NEW YORK MESS

In baseball terminology, Major League teams and their respective farm clubs are called affiliates. A long-standing agreement between the Major Leagues and the National Association of Professional Baseball Clubs (also known as Minor League Baseball) guarantees that every Major League organization will be affiliated with one club at each of the levels of the minor leagues. Those relationships are contractual agreements with lengths of either two or four years.

When I began in baseball, the working agreements were usually one year in length, but baseball as an industry standardized the length and term of the agreements in the 1990s.

We began our affiliation with the New York Mets in 1969. Throughout the next 38 years, the Mets and the Tides were as synonymous as any two clubs possibly could be. Only a few affiliations could even come close to rivaling the New York-Norfolk connection. The teams went through their own individual successes and down periods on the field to varying degrees, but the business relationship never varied. We finished with records at .500 or better 25 times over that period, which is a tremendous record given the transient nature of Triple-A rosters. The Mets went to the World Series four times during that period, winning all the marbles twice. The Tides won the Governor's Cup, the International League's championship, five times.

When people would think of the Mets, they'd think of Norfolk. And vice-versa. It was as solid a relationship as existed in professional baseball. The affiliation survived ownership changes with both clubs.

When the Payson family sold the team to Fred Wilpon and Nelson Doubleday in 1980, our relationship probably was elevated to a new level because they put Frank Cashen in control. We had as close a relationship as two baseball people could have in our respective positions.

The Mets really knew how to take care of their employees. If anything, the Mets in their earlier times were probably too paternalistic. You almost couldn't get fired. They kept people on probably long past their productive lives. If you were a Met, *you were a Met.*

But something started to change around the beginning of the next decade. The owner's son, Jeffrey Wilpon, started getting involved in the Mets' operations. It became a case of "what have you done for me lately?" Jeff Wilpon changed the whole culture of that franchise. He changed the relationship between the major league club and their minor league teams and their minor league people. He ran off more good people than you can believe.

Case in point was something that occurred during Spring Training in 2003, less than a year after Jeff Wilpon was named the Mets' Chief Operating Officer. Rich Miller had spent 31 years with the Mets as a player, coach, scout and manager. He had never received a paycheck from anyone other than the New York Mets. It was one of those days when you're there at five in the morning and still meeting at eight or nine at night. At some point during one of these meetings, Rich closed his eyes, and he got fired. It was something that would have never happened before. When a company loses all feeling of loyalty to employees, it's very hard to continue a relationship.

The Mets had changed so radically. Frank Cashen had built that organization and was responsible for so much of its success. He was still there as a consultant after he was no longer their general manager. Jeff would have an upper level management meeting and not tell Frank about it. *How impersonal is that?*

Cashen, who lives in Port St. Lucie about two miles from the Mets Spring Training and Florida State League complex, suffered a stroke in 2002. They took away his parking pass at their Spring Training ballpark. *How cold is that?*

Our working agreement with the Mets was set to expire after the 2006 season, and most people thought there would just be an automatic renewal. Except possibly Frank Cashen.

We had told the Mets in late April 2006 that we were ready to sign an extension of our working agreement. But we never heard a word from them again about it until August. That's when I got a phone call that Jeff Wilpon, assistant GM John Ricco and farm director Adam Wogan were going to fly down and see a day game and they wanted to talk about the working agreement. The game went extra innings and Ken wasn't expected back until two o'clock. I was in the press box, and they wanted to meet so they could leave. So we ended up meeting in my office.

There were three things we wanted to talk to them about. One was better communication because often times I'd pick up a newspaper and find out that we'd lost a player or gained a player and I never knew anything about it. Jeff said, "Yeah, I have that problem too." I told him how embarrassing it was when I don't know what it going on. He said they'd work on that.

Secondly, we asked them to consider helping us share the cost for taking our team equipment on the commercial regional jets that we use when we fly all over the place. Ordinarily, that's a cost the minor league club incurs, but many major league clubs help their affiliates with this expense, even if there's a ceiling to that number. We didn't get a positive answer to that request. He said, "Well, I've got these guys on a tight budget, but we'll look at it."

Finally, we wanted them to come play an exhibition game at Harbor Park. We didn't get a positive answer to that request either.

At that point, he said, "Well I just thought we'd fly down and get this thing wrapped up."

By this time, Ken had arrived. Ken said, "No. We aren't saying we won't re-sign with you, but we are going to wait until we can talk to other clubs and see what we might want to do."

It was very hard for me to recommend to Ken that we seriously consider leaving after 38 years of a relationship. The baseball world was shocked. But we were doing what we felt was the right thing for our franchise and for our fans.

So we signed on with the Baltimore Orioles. It made sense from a geographical point of view and the new relationship has been good on many levels. But it's hard to look at the relationship we built with the Mets over 38 years and not think of what we went through as a kind of divorce. The pain of the way we were treated still exists.

Our booster club used to always go to Shea Stadium every year. I would arrange the tickets, so I was the contact and I was the guy whose name was in the computer to get all the mail from the Mets ticket department. I guess it was the second year after we broke up with the Mets, and I got the brochure they sent out for the group's renewal. I got some form letter. "Dear Dave Rosenfield, we're looking forward to having your group with us again ..." I took the brochure and sent it back with a little note to Jeff Wilpon. It said, "And I thought you had forgotten me."

Someone in the Mets ticket office probably got fired over that one.

But I digress.

CHAPTER EIGHTEEN

INTROSPECTION

I think down deep, everyone – including me – would like everybody in the world to like them. I think that any of us that have any basis in real life realize that isn't going to happen and you're not even going to get a majority in most cases, let alone unanimity. Does that matter? I don't think so. I'm pretty comfortable with who I am and what I do. And I don't mean my job. I'm referring to what I do with my life. I'm comfortable in my own skin, as wrinkled as it may be. If someone thinks I'm a bad person, I would want that corrected somehow. I don't know how you do that. And I think if you make a big effort to correct that, it would come across as insincere.

I am what I am. I never wanted to hurt anybody. I've tried not to. Maybe I haven't tried hard enough not to. Do I wish I were a different kind of person? Maybe sometimes I do. I know I'm a decent person, and I'm not sure everybody knows that. I wish more people were comfortable with that. I wish that if people don't like me because they think I'm a certain way didn't have that feeling. I've had a funny thought. I would love, if there happens to be a life after death, to hear what people are saying at my funeral. Whether it's just curiosity or vanity or ego, I don't know what it is. I would want them to say, "He was a good guy." And I'd want them to mean it.

If I died tomorrow, I think I have had a wonderful life. I think I lived a lot of years without hurting anybody. At least I've tried not to hurt anyone. And I think I can be proud of that. I think I have contributed to the common good in some ways. I think I've helped a few people along the way. I don't know if there's reincarnation. *Would I want to come back and do it all again?* I'm not sure.

What I really want to know – if there's an afterlife, what am I going to do with three wives? I wouldn't be able to handle it. I can't handle one.

So I decided that after 56 years in the industry and 50 years in Norfolk, it was time to step back a little bit. I didn't step away by any means. Joe Gregory is my successor, and I support him one hundred percent. I really like Joe and think he'll do a very good job with the Tides. I am still involved in the organization and I'm in the office every day, but it's time to pass the reins on to Joe. It's just time.

Joe Gregory

I know I haven't taken very good care of myself. I ought to have every affliction known to man. I ought to be diabetic. I ought to have every kind of thing. But I guess I've been very fortunate. In 2011, I had to have a heart valve replaced, but I was back at work just a few days after the procedure. My health issue from 2011 really didn't contribute to my decision to step back, but it gave me a chance to really start thinking about things in a different way.

I'm more aware of things now. Other than after Mata's death, the whole experience with my heart was the only time in my whole life that I had to think about my own mortality.

I've been fortunate in my career. I've won several Executive of the Year awards. My franchises have won numerous accreditations for being a model franchise. I have been inducted into a handful of Halls of Fame. In 2004, I was named "The King of Baseball" which Minor League Baseball gives to someone every year in recognition of their lifetime commitment to our game. In 2011, Minor League Baseball president Pat O'Conner presented me with a Presidential Citation as a token of respect for my career. All of those honors have been very touching. I was really touched when Norfolk Mayor Paul Fraim announced the City was going to name the street in front of Harbor Park after me and when the Norfolk Sports Club presented me with a lifetime achievement award. When people recognize that you've done something good, that's very gratifying to me.

I've never done this for awards or for money. It's never been a job to me. The greatest thing, even more than winning an award, is when a player or somebody who has worked for me says to me, "You have made a difference in my life." I know that probably sounds out of character from what a lot of people might expect from me. But that is, by far, the most gratifying thing I have ever heard. It comes back to the integrity thing my dad talked about. If you can pass that along to somebody, it makes them a better person.

**Minor League Baseball President Mike Moore
presenting me as the "King of Baseball" in 2004**

My family has been filled with very good people. Most of them have lived very long lives. I have two sisters who are still living well into their nineties. For most of my family members, it's probably due to clean living. For me, it's just luck. The fact I'm still on this side of the grass is amazing. I think about my years in spite of the way I've lived. I've never eaten right. I've never gotten proper rest. No credit to me. I guess I have exceedingly good genes. If there's a hereafter and I see my folks, I will thank them.

I have had a very interesting life. I really enjoy people and I've been privileged to work with and become friends with so many wonderful and interesting folks. I think about all the things I've been able to do and be involved with. It's really been a neat life. Even for a guy some people may consider to be a horse's ass.

But I digress.

EPILOGUE

FROM THE CO-AUTHOR

Over the two years that it took me to write this book, I spent countless hours speaking with Dave's family, friends, colleagues and co-workers. Dave has led such a fascinating life and his own personal story has been really intriguing to me. I have known Dave for many years, but writing this book with him has really given me an opportunity to get to know a side of him that he probably hasn't shown too many people throughout his life.

Finding out who someone *"truly is"* can often be learned through the eyes of people whose lives he's touched along the way. Dave mentioned that he wonders what people will say at his funeral. Nice things are often said about people after they die. I spoke with numerous people from all facets of Dave's life to find out what they have to say about him. It's pretty clear that those who have been allowed to get close to Dave have a consistent theme in their comments – he's the genuine article, one of a kind, a real character:

Charmaine Rosenfield, Dave's wife

Life with Dave has been full of surprises -- all of them blessings, some in disguise. When we were dating, we frequented Japanese restaurants. We'd spend lovely days walking on the cobblestone streets of colonial Williamsburg. We went to shows. We enjoyed the symphony. We loved many of the same things. I wasn't in love with baseball, but Dave was okay with that. We got married. Surprise! No more sushi. The walks stopped. Not quite as many shows. But I did discover his wonderful heart, his kindness, his generosity

and his loving spirit. He continues to be entertaining. His stories, and there are many, are a hoot. And he is a formidable opponent at Scrabble. Dave is as big as life, and I get to see a side of him not many have the opportunity to know. All good things are gifts from God, and Dave is definitely one of them. We are both truly blessed and grateful for it.

Marc Rosenfield, Dave's son

He was always there when I needed him. He was quick to correct your wrong direction if you were getting off course. He was usually always right, even if you didn't want him to be. Baseball wasn't his job; it was his life. If you disagreed with him about a sports fact, don't bet on it with him because you were probably wrong.

Nancy Lund, Dave's sister (12 years older than Dave)

Because he was the youngest of a big family, he was very verbal. He would correct our English, which we thought was so funny coming from this little teeny guy. The other thing that really annoyed us older girls was that he was able to negotiate he was past the very strict bedtime by asking questions of my mother. We were all upset because we thought he was manipulating her. But she always said he was just curious and really wanted to learn about things. He was a very bright child.

Mary L.R. Johnson, Dave's sister (10 years older than Dave)

When David was a little boy, he would push you away and say, 'Self! Self!' He just didn't like having bossy sisters or having people tell him what to do. That has been typical of him throughout his life.

Ken Young, Tides President

Dave Rosenfield has been one of the most trusted people I have known. He imparted so much of his knowledge to me when I could have been looked upon as a threat. Beneath his gruff exterior is a compassionate and gentle individual. (But he doesn't want anyone to know it.) Dave is truly a leader in the sports industry.

Joe Gregory, Dave's successor as Tides General Manager

Working with Rosie is one of the biggest reasons why I came to Norfolk in the first place. When I first met him at Harbor Park I never would have thought I'd be taking over for him one day. I know I've got some big shoes to fill and a lot of people to piss off if I'm going to live up to the legend.

Kenny Magner, Tides grounds keeper

I started working for Dave as a part-time groundskeeper in 1972 when I was 15 years old. At that time, I thought he was a very hard-nosed boss and he intimidated all of us. Over the past 35 years, I have been fired and re-hired by Dave many times. There have been many heated discussions. And there have been times when he has spoken to me like a dad. I have a lot of respect and admiration for Dave. To me, I have the best job in the world and I have Dave to thank.

Heather McKeating, Tides Director of Community Relations

It is very difficult to sum up the substantial impact that Dave Rosenfield has had on my life. I have had the pleasure to learn and work for this man close to 20 years and have valued every conversation we have had over the years whether it stern or friendly!

R.C. Reuteman, former Asst. GM of the Tides

In the fall of 1983, I was sitting in the clubhouse at the old Scottsdale Stadium when the phone rang from a good friend, Steve Schryver, the Seattle Mariners Director of Minor League Operations. I hadn't talked to him in years and he wasn't calling for me. He mentioned that the Tidewater Tides were looking to make a hire and that the guy who ran the Tides was "the best in the business." Little did I know how accurate that assessment was. It was with that coincidental call that I began my education in the baseball world under Dave Rosenfield.

242

After a few rocky years, Dave threw me the keys to the concession stands and told me that I had a new responsibility. I hated the idea, but took on the challenge. I'm not sure that he completely trusted me to get it done but I did. At that point we began a real friendship and trust that lasts to this day, some 30 years later.

I love the guy! Dave has been the most influential person in my life, with all due respect to my Dad and Mom. He took me under his expansive wing and taught me more about life than baseball. That is the true essence of this man. He has always been there to support me in good times and bad. I know who to call when times are tough and I know that I'll get a well-rounded opinion that's straight to the point. There is no bullshit with Rosie. At the same time, I hope that I've helped him through some tough times because he trusted me and I know that he will concur.

Best friend, mentor, educator, second Dad. These thoughts are not enough to explain my relationship with Dave. Beyond that, Dave has been a profound influence on thousands of employees over the years -- whether it's front office, broadcasters, groundskeepers or game day employees. He has made us all successful by allowing us to be surrounded by genius. That's Rosie!

<u>Pat Williams, Orlando Magic Senior Vice President</u>

Dave has a very colorful personality. He was a rock-n-roll cowboy from California. You ask him a question and you get the answer spot-on, without varnish. He loves it when you contest him, when you get in his face. You've got to come back at him.

Dave gets great delight in building careers. He wants his front office guys to go on and do well. Same with broadcasters, coaches, managers and players.

He's always helping them get to the next level. If you're a young guy who wants to build a career in baseball, you'd be wise to go to work for Dave for nothing other than just to get that tutelage. And above all, if Dave becomes a fan of yours, he will battle tooth and nail to help you get opportunities. You definitely want Dave on your resume.

Frank Cashen, former Baltimore Orioles & NY Mets GM

He ran our Triple-A club, but for all intents and purposes he owned that club.

Dave's personality fits his frame. He's larger than life. He's not your average baseball man. Nothing about him is average. He's much above average. He's an astute baseball man. He's far from the average baseball person. He's far from the average personality. I've always considered him not only a friend but a resource.

I leaned on him for help a number of times. He was very helpful and instrumental when we were looking for radio announcers. I have always thought it was just as important to have good radio announcers as it was to have good ballplayers. Dave shared that same belief.

Marty Brennaman, Hall of Fame broadcaster

If it wasn't for Dave, I wouldn't be where I am today. I learned so much from him and he's the reason I ended up in Cincinnati. He was more than just a boss; he was my friend and a mentor.

Pete Van Wieren, former Atlanta Braves broadcaster

Dave was strict. He had a certain level of performance that he expected. I know that there are people who have worked for him who don't care for his discipline, because he had a certain way that things were going to be done. He expected that of you even if it took a 12-hour day.

Clint Hurdle, Pittsburgh Pirates manager

He's a true friend. He's been there for me through a lot of adversity and many challenges. He's from the generation when men put their head down and went hard. He's a magnet – either you like him or you don't. He's honest to a fault. I love Rosie. There's nothing we haven't talked about. There's nothing we haven't shared."

Bobby Valentine, Boston Red Sox manager

When I got to Norfolk for the first time in 1994, I had been fired in Texas. I was down on the mat. Rosie became everything to me. Rosie became my mentor both personally and professionally. He became kind of a father/guidance figure. He was a real great support system. I was amazed at the knowledge of baseball that he had and his warm heartedness. He was so personable. He was so engaging that even an extrovert like myself felt like he was the man to see whenever I had a question or lost a couple of games in a row.

He's a special individual. Very, very few people have the traits that Rosie possesses. The intelligence, the personal skills, the social skills and the knowledge and love for the game of baseball. When I went back to Norfolk the second time in 1996, he was such a security blanket for me. He helped me get my confidence level to where it needed to be to make that next step. He convinced the Mets that they could trust the decision to hire me as their manager.

He's one of the first guys I like to inform about anything new happening in my life. I always care and think about him, and I know he's thinking about me.

<u>Ron Washington, Texas Rangers manager</u>

 *Dave is a class guy. He is very caring and family-oriented. He certainly made you feel welcome. I've never seen him have a bad day. His job was to forge relationships. I've been invited into his home. His wife Charmaine and my wife are very good friends. He certainly tried to make my transition from playing baseball to being a coach very comfortable for me. That played a part in the type of individual that I've become in dealing with players. You want to treat people the way you want to be treated, and that's one thing that Dave did very, very well. He believes in helping people become better players and coaches, but also in helping them become better men.*

I trust his opinion and will call him about players. We still talk every four months or so. Dave is a friend who just happens to run a team. I think of Dave as a kind of father-figure. He has always cared about people and I hold him dear to my heart.

Davey Johnson, Washington Nationals manager

Dave's fun to talk to and he's fun to be around. He does a great job year in and year out. I think he's one of the most respected GM's in baseball, no doubt in my mind. If you know Dave, he makes you feel important. He makes you feel appreciated. He makes everybody around him feel comfortable. I compare him a lot with Pat Gillick, the way he treats people. He always wanted to help people and was always aware of what was going on around him with the people who worked for him. That's an attribute of a great executive. I always cherished his friendship.

Sam Perlozzo, Philadelphia Phillies coach

Coming back from a stint in Japan in 1980, I landed a job as player-coach for Tidewater in 1981 with Rosie. Trying to give it one more chance as a player, I ended up coaching more than playing. I was at the crossroads of my playing days and Dave told me I would be a good coach and to think about it. Through his recommendation, I took a job with the Mets as a minor league manager and now have 25 consecutive years in the major leagues. Thanks to his assistance, I am where I am today. He's a genuine personality, a hard worker, and great baseball man and, more importantly, a very good friend.

Rick Dempsey, Baltimore Orioles broadcaster

Dave was one of the pioneers of minor league baseball and was one of the most respected general managers in the game.

Where Dave sticks out is as an evaluator of baseball players because he played the game also. He's always been that guy that I go to, even to this day, to ask him about players. His opinions about talent are invaluable. He's like a scout for major league clubs. What I really like about him is that he realizes you have to watch a player for a long time before you get a true evaluation about whether or not he can play in the major leagues.

He's as solid a businessman as you're ever going to be around in the minor leagues. He's really good at what he does.

He'd always come into my office after games and we'd talk. He wasn't afraid to tell me about my own pluses and minuses because he knew I wanted to move up the ladder to the big leagues. He's been a tremendous supporter.

Randy Mobley, International League president

Dave Rosenfield is a Minor League Baseball icon and the International League is fortunate to have had him helping to guide its path for decades. Every organization should be so lucky as to have an individual with such experience and dedication to serve as a constant resource. The impact Dave has had on individuals both on and off the field is immeasurable and I for one will forever be grateful to have had the opportunity to learn from him, work with him and call him a mentor, colleague and friend.

Pat O'Conner, Minor League Baseball president

In the nearly 30 years I have known Dave there has been one constant. He has always had time for me and the hundreds of executives like me that consider him a friend, colleague and mentor. A conversation with Rosie is an education every single time. From the latest industry doings to a great story, time with Dave Rosenfield is time well spent. It is an honor for me to know such a baseball icon.

Mike Tamburro, Pawtucket Red Sox president

An industry giant who's as intertwined with the game of baseball as brush back pitches and foul lines, Dave Rosenfield cares deeply about the International League and this great game of ours. He is owed generations of thanks by those who profited by the time and wisdom he was always too willing to share. A transformational figure, Minor League Baseball is a better place because of him.

Lou Schwechheimer, Pawtucket Red Sox general manager

As a 21-year old kid starting a career in baseball I found myself sitting alone at a table poolside after a long day of baseball meetings at George Steinbrenner's Royce Hotel.

At a table nearby lifelong friends, their bond forged by carrying the International League on their backs for decades, was lighting up the night with one great story after another. Their passion and camaraderie was evident by the laughter and shared stories of Satchel Paige and Hank Aaron and Max Patkin and life in the IL during the 50s and

60s. At the center of it all was Dave Rosenfield. Noticing the rookie alone with his briefcase I was summoned to his table of legends by the wave of an arm. With that simple act of kindness 30 years ago, Dave Rosenfield welcomed me to his world.

And what a world it has been. In the decades since we have witnessed the renaissance of Minor League Baseball. The International League has grown and beautiful new ballparks have graced the landscape because men like Dave kept the game alive, did the heavy lifting and paved the road for all of us to travel.

Ken Schnacke, Columbus Clippers President & GM

I have had the honor and privilege of not only knowing, but getting to work with Dave over the past 35 years. He is extremely knowledgeable about baseball, both the game on the field and also 'the business of baseball' off the field. He is one of a very few people who can assemble a league baseball schedule, a talent that is easy to overlook and harder to appreciate. I have found Dave's wit and sense of humor to match up well with mine, which permits us to have some pretty interesting and funny discussions on an ongoing basis. All-in-all, he is one GREAT baseball executive.

Bill Luther, ret. Director of Civic Facilities – City of Norfolk

I have always found Dave to be a hard-nosed, fair professional business man who will listen to other's opinions. Dave is the main reason the original Tidewater Professional Sports, the Norfolk Tides, and Harbor Park have been a success. Not many professionals could have

guided an organization for fifty plus years and have had Dave's success. Dave has never compromised his principles. I am grateful for the opportunity to work with him and learn from him in both my professional and personal life. Dave is a good person and a good friend.

Jack Ankerson, longtime friend

Dave Rosenfeld and I have been good friends for over 35 years. That's a long time and we have certainly had our differences, but all resolved amicably! Basically, we have both spent our whole lives in the business of sports, and thus, I have nothing but the greatest amount of respect and admiration for his lifetime achievements in baseball. The fact that he has served over 50 consecutive years with the same franchise is truly remarkable."

Tony Mercurio, Norfolk sports talk show host and Tides broadcaster

Dave Rosenfield has been one of the most important people in my life. He has been like a second father to me. There is no one in the business world that I respect more than Dave. He is the best at what he does and is probably one of the smartest people that I have ever known. Dave saved baseball several times in the Hampton Roads area; I don't know what would have happened to professional baseball in our area if it weren't for the efforts and wisdom of Dave Rosenfield. Simply put, Dave has meant the world to this area and to me."

Blake Cullen, former owner of Norfolk Admirals Hockey Club

I have known Dave since my first days in professional baseball, but we really came together when I decided I wanted to bring hockey to Norfolk in 1989. We called on Dave to let him know there would be competition in the market. He not only welcomed us, he helped me at every turn. He even wrote to his season ticket holders on my behalf. He is a true sportsman and a great friend.

John Rhamstine, Director of Seven Venues, City of Norfolk

I first met Dave Rosenfield in 1989 with me as an eager Assistant Director for Facilities in Norfolk, VA. Dave's reputation preceded him as a curmudgeon type of character who liked to yell and scream a lot, and Dave could certainly do that. However, over the years, I became very close friends with Dave and he is really anything but what his reputation is. He is very intelligent, deeply thoughtful and extremely caring for the people he respects. There is not anything he would not do for a friend. He is also probably one of the best writers I have met. He has a gift for the English language.

Then-Senator Barack Obama poses with Ken Young (left) and Dave when he came to Harbor Park for a campaign speech one week prior to being elected US President in 2008.

INDEX

"Alfred Hitchcock Presents" (television), 16
"All My Sons" (television), 16
"Batman" (television), 27
"Becker" (television), 165
"Bull Durham" (movie), 129
"Cheers" (television), 164
"City Beneath the Sea" (movie), 65
"Dharma & Greg" (television), 165
"Everybody Loves Raymond" (television), 165
"Frasier" (television), 165
"Hollywood Smarty Party" (radio), 27, 29, 67
"Mannix" (television), 35
"M*A*S*H" (teleivision), 164
"Monsieur Verdoux" (movie), 16
"Quiz Kids" (radio), 27
"The Cisco Kid" (television), 16
"The Fugitive" (television), 63
"The Jeffersons" (television), 164
"The Killers" (movie), 16
"The Loretta Young Show" (television), 16
"The Mayor of the Town" (radio), 16
"The Music Man" (movie), 17
"The Pride of the Yankees" (movie), 1, 27, 27, 194
"The Simpsons" (television), 164
"The Strangler of the Swamp" (movie), 17
"The Twilight Zone" (television), 16
"Time for Elizabeth" (theater), 16
"Wings" (television), 165

11th Naval District, 51-53

Aaron, Hank, 190
Abiouness, Al, 222
Admiralty Hotel, 146-147
Albini, John, 34
Albuquerque Isotopes, 165
Alden, John, 65
Allegheny Airlines, 156
Amateur Athletic Union, 157
American Association, 102
American Basketball Association, 150-151
American Hockey League, 152
Anderson, Sparky, 32-33, 63
Ankerson, Jack, 152-153, 153, 251, 251
Appling, Luke, 26
Army, 45-47, 52
Arndt, Johnny, 47
Atlanta Braves, 162
Atlanta Crackers, 102
Atlanta Hawks, 163
Atlantic Coast League, 134
Autry, Gene, 22
Awards received, 235

Backman, Wally, 183
Baker, Art, 27-28, 28, 63, 67
Bakersfield Bears, 84, 94
Bakersfield Boosters, 74, 77, 79, 82, 83
Ball, Lucille, 65
Ball, Suzan, 65, 65
Baltimore Bullets, 47
Baltimore Orioles, 71, 121, 165, 174, 177, 187, 196, 230
Bangel, Herb, 111
Barbaro, 127
Barger, Stan, 214-215
Barty, Billy, 66-67, 66, 90-91
Bauer, Hank, 122, 138, 146-149, 147
Beane, Billy, 183
Bianchi, Al, 151-152, 158
Binghamton Mets, 181, 219
Binghamton Triplets, 161
Blanton, Cy, 23
Bochy, Bruce, 183
Bonko, Larry, 123
Boston Red Sox, 197
Bradford, Buddy, 121
Brennaman, Marty, 159, 159-161, 244, 244
Brennaman, Thom, 161
Bristol, Dave, 99, 100, 100
Britain, Jake (grandson), 217
Britain (Barger), Samantha, 211, 217
Broadwater, Charlie, 176
Brock, Walter, 110-111
Brooklyn Dodgers, 101
Brown, Bobby, 177-179, 178, 193
Bubash, Bob, 90
Buckner, Bill, 197
Burbrink, Nelson, 169-170

Burger King, 176
Burning baseball field, 92

Cal Poly San Luis Obispo, 34
Cal State Los Angeles (aka LA State), 45, 59-61, 73
California League, 42, 74, 77, 88, 90, 101
Campbell, Nolan, 88
Captain Kangaroo, 196
Caray, Skip, 162
Carolina League, 109-111, 115, 122-123, 177
Carradine, John, 16
Cashen, Frank, 174-175, 175, 176, 197, 219-220, 229, 244, 244
Champion, Billy, 179
Chandler, Happy, 131
Chaplin, Charlie, 16-17
Charleston Charlies, 195
Charmaine (wife), 211-217, 216, 239, 239-240
Chavez Ravine, 60
Chesapeake, 143, 185
Chicago Bears, 60, 141
Chicago Bulls, 127
Chicago Cubs, 21, 30, 51, 84, 86, 154
Chicago White Sox, 121
Cincinnati Reds, 33, 89, 160
Cincinnati Royals, 158
Clarkson, Art, 172
Clay, Cassius, 102
Clayton, Cotton, 121
Clemente, Roberto, 39
Cobb, Bob, 22
Communist Party, 12
Connors, Mike, 35
Consolo, Billy, 32

Continental Football League, 131-132, 172

Cook, Gene, 200

Cooper, Alvin, 114

Corrales, Pat, 102

Costas, Bob, 165

Croft, Douglas, 27

Cuba, 99-100

Cubbage, Mike, 183

Cullen, Blake, 154-155, 155, 166-167, 252, 252

Current, Rick, 123-124, 154

Curtis, Tony, 65

Darling, Ron, 183

Davalillo, Vic, 99

Davidson, Teddy, 99

Davis, Dick, 107-108, 108, 111, 122, 129, 132, 137-139, 149-152, 189, 219-221

Daytona Beach News Journal, 12, 61

Dean, Dizzy, 51

Dedeaux, Rod, 34

Dempsey, Rick, 71, 199, 199, 248, 248

Detroit Red Wings, 152

Detroit Tigers, 30

Detroit/Ft. Wayne Pistons, 46

Dihigo, Marty, 100

Donohoe, Doss, 53, 55-56

Dorsey High School, 31

Doubleday, Nelson, 174, 228

Driving a guy to jail, 71-72

Drysdale, Don, 60

Dykstra, Lenny, 183

Ear infection, 54-55

East Coast Hockey League, 154, 166

Eastern League, 126, 161

Eastwick, Rawley, 177

Eby, Don, 47, 49-50

Eisenhower, Dwight, 53

Erving, Julius, 150, 150

Espinosa, Nino, 156

Eugene Larks, 42, 42

Fairfax High School, 63

Far West League, 40, 42

Feller, Bob, 130-131

Fidrych, Mark, 156

Fletcher, Art, 25, 26

Florida State League, 102, 120, 229

Foreman, Earl, 150

Fort Dix Army Hospital, 54

Fox, Marshall, 102, 105

Fraim, Paul, 235

Frank D. Lawrence Stadium, 115, 116-117, 136, 140

Frankland, Jackie (wife), 71

Frazier, Joe, 156

Fresno Cardinals, 81

Friedman, Gerald, 150

Gaedel, Eddie, 126

Garcea, Mark, 222

Gardenhire, Ron, 183

Garland, Ed, 111

Gehrig, Lou, 1, 27

Georgia-Florida League, 40

Gervin, George, 150

Getting shot at, 68-70

Gilhousen, Rosey, 74, 76

Gilmore Field, 22

Gionfriddo, Al, 101

Giordano, Tommy, 87
Given, Sam, 15
Glascock, Joy, 90
Gooden, Dwight, 183
Gorman, Lou, 187
Grable, Betty, 31
Grant, M. Donald, 137-138, 144
Greensboro Yankees, 169
Gregory, Joe, 234, 234, 241, 241
Gretzky, Wayne, 167
Griffin, Merv, 31
Groat, Dick, 52

Haak, Howie, 39
Hamilton, Milo, 162
Hampton Roads, 185
Hans, Roland, 47
Harazin, Al, 176, 197, 219-221
Harbor Park, 194, 203, 205, 220,
    225, 230
Harkins, Heather, 180
Harper, Tommy, 99
Harvey, Doug, 89
Harvey, Paul, 127
Harwell, Ernie, 163
Hathaway, Len, 163
Helms, Tommy, 99
Herman, Babe, 74, 76, 86-87, 87
Herzog, Whitey, 142-144, 143,
    148-149
Hiller, Chuck, 146
Hodges, Gil, 122
Hollywood Stars, 21-22
Hoover Metropolitan Stadium,
    172
Houston Astros, 197
Houston Colt .45s, 135
Howard, Charlie, 195
Hudson, Rock, 65

Huggins, Alan, 145
Hughes, George, 132-134
Hunter, Catfish , 190, 194
Hurdle, Clint, 201, 201-203, 245,
    245
Hussman, Dick, 83, 84
Hyatt Corporation, 188

Illinois-Indiana-Iowa League, 99
International League, 102, 127,
    135-136, 149, 155, 157, 160,
    173, 195, 200, 202, 227
Isringhausen, Jason, 184

Jackson, Roy, 127
Jacobsen, Howard, 213
James, Harry, 31, 63
Janssen, David, 63, 63, 65
Jessup, Bill, 109-112
John Burroughs Junior High
    School, 31, 63
Johnson, Davey, 199, 199, 202,
    247, 247
Johnson, Ernie, 162
Johnson, Howard, 184
Johnson, Johnny, 186
Johnstone, Jay, 177
Jones, Al, 118, 120
Jones, Joe, 121
Junior World Series, 156

Kaatz, Bud, 158-159
Kansas City Athletics, 110, 119
Kansas City Royals, 135, 171, 201
Kansas City-Omaha Kings, 158
Kaplan, Sheldon, 22
Kelly, Dave, 41, 42
Kentucky Colonels, 152
Killebrew, Harmon, 190

Killing a woman, 85
King of Baseball, 235, 236
Kingman, Dave, 190
Kittle, Hub, 40, 41
Klamath Falls Gems, 40, 40
Korean War, 45
Kowalski, Art, 126
Kranepool, Ed, 194
Kuhn, Bowie, 174
Kurt, Lindy, 119-120

LA High School, 64
Landon, Michael, 71
Lawrence, Frank D., 5, 115-116
Leigh, Janet, 65
Leishman, Eddie, 124
Leonard, Buck, 124
Levine, Ken, 163-165
Lewis, Bill, 107-108, 111
Lima, Jose, 184
Linton, Dan, 40
Liston, Sonny, 102
Long Island University, 47
Long, Richard, 65
Los Alamitos Naval Air Station,
    46-48
Los Angeles Angels, 21, 52, 135
Los Angeles City College, 37, 45,
    66
Los Angeles Coliseum, 196
Los Angeles Dodgers, 60, 165,
    196
Los Angeles Times, 21, 21, 34
Louisville Redbirds, 189
Loyola University, 47
Luther, Bill, 167, 250, 250
Lynch, Ed, 183
Lyon, Estelle Therese (stage
    name), 16, 116

Lyons, Ted, 26

MacDonald, Ronald, 176
Mack, Connie, 26
Maduro, Bobby, 100
Magner, Kenny, 172, 242, 242
Major League Baseball expansion,
    135
Marriages, 71, 83, 214
Marshall, Valerie, 105, 144-145,
    181-182
Martin, Freddy, 31
Marunda, Bill, 50
Marx, Groucho, 16
Mata (wife), 83, 84, 85, 85, 90, 99,
    101, 103, 117, 119, 173, 186,
    188-189, 196, 206-212, 215,
    235
Matlack, Jon, 184
Matson, Larry, 163
Mayflower, 65
Mays, Willie, 52, 144
McClelland, George, 162
McCullough, Ann, 198
McCullough, Clyde, 141, 141-143,
    198-199
McDonald, Bill, 102
McGranery, James P., 115
McIlvaine, Joe, 176
McKeating, Heather, 180, 242,
    242
McKeon, Jack, 178, 197-198, 198
McKeon, Kasey, 179
McLain, Denny, 172
Meatloaf, 55-56
Melrose Avenue Elementary
    School, 27
Mercurio, Tony, 165-168, 251,
    251

Met Park, 140, 144, 144, 169-170
Metheny, Bud, 193
Midwest League, 102
Milkes, Marvin, 81
Miller Carlson, 73
Miller, Rich, 228
Milner, John, 148
Milwaukee Braves, 87
Minor League Baseball, 76, 99,
    101, 186, 227, 235
Miss Universe, 28, 71
Missouri Valley Conference, 180
Mobley, Randy, 174, 200, 200,
    248, 248
Montreal Expos, 135
Moore, Johnny, 74, 76
Moore, Mike, 236
Motor scooter accident, 30
Murphy, Johnny, 137-139
Murtaugh, Danny, 122

Nagourney, Ed, 190
National Association, 101, 185-
    187, 227
National Brewing Company, 174
National Football League, 131-
    132, 142
National Semi-Pro Tournament,
    51
Navy, 45-47, 50, 52, 59, 61
New England Patriots, 158
New York Giants, 25
New York Islanders, 158
New York Mets, 119, 121, 135,
    136-144, 146, 148, 156, 169-
    170, 174, 177-178, 196-197,
    202, 219-224, 227-231
New York Nets, 158
New York White Roses, 126

New York Yankees, 21, 25, 158,
    161, 169, 177-178, 193
Newport News Baby Dodgers, 110
Newport News Pilots, 110
Newport News Shipbuilders, 109
Nike, 223
Norfolk Admirals, 155, 206
Norfolk All-Stars, 109
Norfolk Clam Eaters, 109
Norfolk Jewels, 109
Norfolk Mary Janes, 109
Norfolk Neptunes, 132, 134, 134
Norfolk Skippers, 109
Norfolk Sports Club, 32, 194, 235
Norfolk Tars, 109
Norfolk Tides, 109, 223, 223
Norfolk, City of, 205, 220, 235
Northampton High School, 177
Notre Dame, 166
Nottle, Ed, 118

Oakland A's, 158, 160
Obama, Barack, 252
O'Conner, Pat, 235, 249, 249
O'Konek, Holly (granddaughter),
    217
Old Dominion Baseball Clinic,
    190, 193
Old Dominion University, 145,
    190, 193, 212
Olsen, Smokey, 171
O'Neill, Buck, 131
Orlando Magic, 220, 243
Orosco, Jessie, 184
Orowitz, Evelyn, 71
Owens, Paul, 88-89, 89, 118, 119,
    123-124, 135

Pacific Coast League, 21, 127

Pantuso, Vince, 220
Pasadena Playhouse, 16
Patkin, Max, 128, 130
Payson, Joan, 137-138, 174
Peoria Caterpillars, 49
Perlozzo, Sam, 183, 247, 247
Peters, Hank, 119
Peterson, Harding, 195
Philadelphia 76ers, 127
Philadelphia Phillies, 25, 39, 86, 88, 123
Phoenix Suns, 159
Piggy Wiggly Grocery Stores, 11, 14
Pine Grove Dairy, 159
Pittsburgh Pirates, 39, 101, 121, 158, 195
Pittsburgh Steelers, 133
Portsmouth Browns, 109
Portsmouth Chamber of Commerce, 109-110
Portsmouth Cubs, 109
Portsmouth Merrimacs, 109
Portsmouth Pirates, 109
Portsmouth Stadium, 115-117
Portsmouth Truckers, 109
Portsmouth, 91, 103
Postove, Harry, 198
Preston, Art, 60
Pritzker, Bob, 188

Quinn, Anthony, 65
Quinn, John, 124, 135

Radenbaugh, Faith, 28-29, 67, 71
Rathbun, Bob, 163-164, 188
Regan, Danny, 39, 74, 86
Reichle, Art, 36-37, 41

Reutemann, R.C., 181, 181, 242, 242
Reyes, Jose, 184
Rhamstine, John, 252, 252
Ricco, John, 229
Rices-Nachman, 190
Ripken, Cal, 190
Robertson, Bill, 92
Robinson, Brooks, 190
Robinson, Jackie, 1, 32, 32, 63
Rochester Red Wings, 155-156
Rocky Mount, NC, 124
Roges, Al, 47
Rooney, Art, 133, 133-134
Rosenfelder, Moses, (great grandfather) 12
Rosenfield, Betsy (daughter-in-law), 207, 209, 217
Rosenfield, Dellie (sister), 11, 217
Rosenfield, Estelle (mom), 10, 13, 13, 16, 18, 54, 60, 68, 116
Rosenfield, Jo (sister), 11, 12, 32, 61
Rosenfield, Julie (sister), 11, 24, 217
Rosenfield, Julius (grandfather), 12
Rosenfield, Keren (granddaughter), 206
Rosenfield, Leon (brother), 11, 11, 21, 22, 217
Rosenfield, Leon (Pop), 10, 10, 11, 13, 12-15, 18, 37, 54, 61
Rosenfield, Louise (sister), 11, 54
Rosenfield, Marc (son), 85, 90-91, 91, 99, 101, 103, 205-209, 206, 217, 240, 240
Rosenfield, Mary (Mary Johnson, sister), 11, 14, 217, 241, 241

Rosenfield, Nancy (Nancy Lund, sister), 11, 217, 240, 240
Ruth, Babe, 100, 193
Ryan, Joe, 102-103, 105-106

Sam Lynn Park, 119
San Antonio Spurs, 152
San Diego Padres, 22, 135, 178, 198
San Diego State, 60, 90
San Francisco Giants, 196, 198
Saunders, Clarence, 10
Schedule writing, 111-113
Schnacke, Ken, 200, 250, 250
Schryver, Steve, 202
Schwechheimer, Lou, 200, 249, 249
Scope Arena, 167, 187
Seattle Mariners, 165, 178
Seattle Pilots, 81, 135
Selling cars, 95
Senger, Charlie, 127
Service Champions of the World, 52, 53, 118
Shamsky, Art, 99
Shea Stadium, 137, 196-197, 230
Sierra, Ruben, 184
Simmons, Al, 26
Simone, John, 128
Simone, Tex, 128, 200
Simpson, Homer, 164
Singleton, Ken, 193, 201
Sisler, George, 160, 200
Skaugstad, David, 90
Skinner, Denzil, 187-188
Slowes, Charlie, 165
Smith, A. Ray, 187-189
Smith, Sam, 106
Socci, Bob, 163

South Atlantic League, 102, 105-106
Southern Hockey League, 153
Spartanburg Phillies, 126
Sports Illustrated, 202
Springfield Isotopes, 164
St. Louis Browns, 42
St. Lucie Mets, 202
Stahl, Larry, 119
Star & Crescent Society, 64
Starr, Kay, 64, 64
Stearns, John, 194
Stengel, Casey, 122, 138, 146
Stockton Ports, 41
Storen, Mike, 151
Strawberry, Darryl, 183
Stroud, Ed, 121
Superdome, 188
Syracuse Sky Chiefs, 163

Tamburro, Mike, 200, 249, 249
Tampa Tarpons, 102
Tepedino, Frank, 170
The Bakersfield Californian, 93
The Ledger-Star, 123, 162
The Virginian Pilot, 162
Three-I League, 99, 101
Tidewater Community Baseball, 111
Tidewater Community College, 214
Tidewater Professional Sports, 132, 140, 221-222
Tidewater Sharks, 152, 153
Tidewater Tides, 102-103, 106, 118, 130, 136, 155, 176, 195, 202, 207, 222
Tobias, Sam, 74
Toledo Mud Hens, 161

Toma, George, 171
Topeka Reds, 96, 99, 104, 110
Toronto Blue Jays, 178
Town Point Park, 205
Trautman, George, 101
Triandos, George, 40
Triandos, Gus, 40
Triple-A Baseball, 140
Triumph Books, 163
Tudor, John, 191
Turner, Bulldog, 142
Turner, Ted, 162
Twardzick, Dave, 145

UCLA, 12, 27, 32, 34-37, 75, 214
Uplinger, Hal, 47
USC, 34, 47

Valentine, Bobby, 199, 199, 245,
    245
Valentino, Dom, 158
Van Horne, Dave, 157
Van Wieren, Pete, 161-163, 163,
    245, 245
Veeck, Bill, 126
Verdi, Frank, 168, 168-174, 174
Verdi, Pauline, 173
Virginia Beach Sports Club, 194
Virginia Beach, 142, 185, 190,
    205
Virginia Military Institute, 107
Virginia Squires, 150, 150-152,
    158
Viverito, Frank, 180
Viverito, Patty, 180
Volume Services, 220
Voorhees, Amy (granddaughter),
    217

Wagner, Dick, 160-161
Waisenen, Linda, 180
Washington Nationals, 128
Washington Redskins, 163
Washington Senators, 110, 121,
    135, 165
Washington, Ron, 183, 246, 246
Weaver, Earl, 100
Weiss, George, 138, 138-139
Western Carolina League, 126
White, Ray, 198
William & Mary, 107, 133, 193
Williams, Bobby, 128
Williams, Pat, 126-128, 135, 224,
    243, 243
Wilpon, Fred, 174, 228
Wilpon, Jeff, 228-231
Wilson, Mookie, 192, 192
Winter Meetings, 33, 86, 96, 101,
    106, 121, 131, 160, 178, 186,
    188, 224
Wogan, Adam, 229
Wood, Dick, 109, 111
Wooden, John, 35
World Series, 21, 30-31, 51, 146,
    196-197, 227
World War II, 132
Wright, David, 184

Yardley, George, 46, 46, 48-49
Yost, Ned, 184
Young, Ken, 165, 220-224, 222,
    229-230, 241, 241, 253
Youth Baseball Fund, 194

Zinzendorf Hotel, 113-114, 113
Zodda, Vic, 110-111